Cultivating Professional Identity in Design

Cultivating Professional Identity in Design is a nuanced, comprehensive companion for designers across disciplines honing their identities, self-perception, personal strengths, and essential attributes. Designers' identities, whether rooted in education, workforce training, digital technology, arts and graphics, built environment, or other fields, are always evolving, influenced by any combination of current mindset, concrete responsibilities, team dynamics, and more. Applicable to designers of all contexts, this inspiring yet rigorous book guides practitioners and students to progress with ten key traits: empathy, uncertainty, creativity, ethics, diversity/equity/inclusion, reflection, learning, communication, collaboration, and decision-making.

Though it details a complete journey from start to finish, this book acknowledges the varying paths of designers' roles and is structured for a flexible, highly iterative reading experience. Segments can be read individually or out of order and revisited for new insights. Current and future stages of development – education experience, early-career opportunities, mid-career accomplishments, and/or career transitions – are factored in without hierarchy. Specific takeaways, activities, and reflection exercises are intended to work across settings and levels of experience. Design hopefuls and experts alike will find a new way to participate in and persevere through their work.

Monica W. Tracey is Professor in the Learning Design and Technology Program in the Division of Administrative and Organizational Studies in the College of Education at Wayne State University, U.S.A.

John Baaki is Associate Professor, Graduate Program Director, and Graduate Certificate Program in Human Performance Technology Coordinator in the Department of STEM Education & Professional Studies at Old Dominion University, U.S.A.

Cultivating Professional Identity in Design

Empathy, Creativity, Collaboration, and Seven More Cross-Disciplinary Skills

Monica W. Tracey and John Baaki

Routledge
Taylor & Francis Group

NEW YORK AND LONDON

Cover image: © Getty Images

First published 2023
by Routledge
605 Third Avenue, New York, NY 10158

and by Routledge
4 Park Square, Milton Park, Abingdon, Oxon, OX14 4RN

Routledge is an imprint of the Taylor & Francis Group, an informa business

© 2023 Monica W. Tracey and John Baaki

Library of Congress Cataloging-in-Publication Data
A catalog record for this title has been requested

ISBN: 978-1-032-18564-4 (hbk)
ISBN: 978-1-032-15314-8 (pbk)
ISBN: 978-1-003-25515-4 (ebk)

DOI: 10.4324/9781003255154

Typeset in Gill Sans Std
by KnowledgeWorks Global Ltd.

This book is dedicated to you, Ank,

with love.

CONTENTS

PREFACE

The one thing we are sure of as designers is our professional identity is constantly emerging. From our work in business and industry to our academic journeys preparing the next generation, our view of design and being a designer continues to evolve. To design is to create, so we have created this journey of *Cultivating Designer Professional Identity*.

Overview of the Book

This book is your journey map to cultivating your designer professional identity. Begin by taking in the welcome segment, then you are free to chart your journey as you wish. Visit any segment of this book as often as you like during your journey. Each one includes activities you can do to cultivate your designer professional identity. Whether you are new to the field, or have been a designer for a long time, there is something in each segment for you. Take your time on this journey, revisit your favorite spots over and over again. Below we give you a summary of each segment.

Empathy segment introduces empathy as a design approach. This segment offers perspectives on empathy as an inborn ability as well as a learned skill. This discussion includes practical activities to aid designers in developing a designer professional identity that is imbued with empathy for the audience of focus, empathy for self, and empathy for the localized context of use.

Uncertainty segment explores uncertainty as both an essential and routine part of design and provides a framework for developing a designer professional identity which embraces uncertainty. This segment offers perspectives on designers' relationships to uncertainty including practical techniques to recognize, accept, and embrace uncertainty in design as necessary for creativity, innovation, and curiosity. This discussion includes an exploration of the types of uncertainty and their impacts on understanding, behavior, and emotions.

Creativity segment explores creativity in designer professional identity as a combination of internal processes and external practices that are environmentally situated, embodied in actions, and cultivated through purposeful nurturing. This segment offers perspectives on expanding sources of inspiration as the designer professional identity develops, while encouraging designers to recognize emotions as an integral part of their creative professional identity. This discussion includes techniques to cultivate designer creativity, harness emotions as a source of innovation, and integrate creativity into collaborative design work.

Ethics segment challenges readers to consider design's impact on the social, political, and natural environment. This segment offers perspectives on ethical design as it aims to promote well-being, enables people to live as they like in a sustainable way, and enhances social innovation. This segment offers perspectives on the development of ethical designer professional identity as a resolution of the internal intentions and external manifestations of design. This discussion includes a new conception of design that is focused on the audience, situated, interactive, collaborative, participatory, and focused on the production of the human experience and life itself.

Diversity, equity, and inclusion segment explores design as an expression of radical empathy that moves audiences and designers toward actions that promote more just outcomes. This segment offers perspectives on designer introspection, interaction, and intention to identify the most critical forces to form a localized context of use in designing with diversity, equity, and inclusion in mind. This discussion includes perspectives on design's ability to transform situations of inequity, lack of diversity, and exclusion by influencing our everyday choices.

Reflection segment explores the role of reflective conversations between the designer, the design problem, and tentative solutions. This segment encourages the development of a designer professional identity as an explicitly reflective practice while implicit reflective skills are nurtured through experiences. This discussion explores reflection as a conceptualization of personal and internal knowledge construction through recursive considerations and interpretations of experiences and beliefs.

Learning segment explores design as an active process of learning and learning as a vital process of developing a designer professional identity. This segment offers perspectives on formal education, practice, and reflection as interrelated components of learning and development. This discussion includes perspectives on failure as a vital opportunity for personal and professional growth.

Communication segment provides an overview of communication and its reciprocal relationship to designer professional identity development. In addition to providing insight into different theories of communication, this segment offers practical tools to improve listening and communication skills that contribute positively to collaborative design processes. This discussion includes insights into the basic forms of communication, the role of listening in effective design communication in, and the essential communication functions for design communication.

Collaboration segment explores design as a fundamentally collaborative effort, where designers interact with others' skills, ideas, experiences, and opinions in pursuit of a common goal. This segment offers perspectives on the impact of collaboration on creativity, and the relationship between collaboration and designer professional identity development. This discussion includes examples of intentional efforts that can be used to and support the formation of collaborative relationships that contribute to the development of a collaborative designer professional identity.

Decision-making segment is a synthesis of creativity, uncertainty, and reflection that explores the web of interrelated decisions that build a meaningful design and designer professional identity. This discussion includes perspectives on decision-making as iterations that flow from abstract possibilities to practical imperatives in realizing a design. This segment includes practical examples of designers embracing uncertainty to make creative decisions that are enriched by careful reflection.

Identity appropriately refers to *becoming*, meaning that your work in cultivating your professional identity is constant. We wish you the very best on your journey. Keep designing!

Monica W. Tracey
John Baaki

ACKNOWLEDGMENTS

It is difficult to mention all of those who have contributed to our designer professional identity but there are a few who have truly cultivated our identity development.

Our design students surprise, question, and push us to continue to develop. We grow alongside and are grateful for each and every one of them. There are too many designers in this field to acknowledge, but we would be truly remiss if we did not recognize Nigel Cross and Kees Dorst. Their introduction to *Design Thinking* came at a critical crossroad on our designer development journey.

We could not have completed this work had it not been for Beth Bailey and Yibo Fan, who read every segment, providing feedback and formatting. To our families and friends who listened to us, encouraged us, and were patient with us as we created this journey, thank you. To the staff at Routledge especially Daniel Schwartz, who trusted that our vision would come to fruition, many thanks for believing in us. Finally, we thank Steve Jobs, the ultimate designer, whose genius continues to inspire us.

WELCOME

THE JOURNEY BEGINS

Makayla achieved her dream, graduating with an undergraduate degree in secondary education. While teaching math in a middle school during the day, she continued to be a student at night, completing a graduate degree in instructional design. After three years, with her degree completed, Makayla left her middle school classroom and landed her first corporate instructional design position with a design firm. In the first week in her new role, she found herself pouring through her course books, hesitant to apply the design process she learned in the classroom. Makayla questioned herself and her ability as an instructional designer. "What is holding me back?" she wondered. "Why can't I figure out where to begin?" "Can I really design?"

Your designer professional identity will emerge from your education, professional development, and career progression.

Centuries ago, design was conveyed from master to apprentice. Ordinary teachers taught design fundamentals while the master taught the apprentice how to use the knowledge they had acquired. The role of the apprentice was to obtain competencies while the role of the master was to direct the apprentice in developing their professional identity. Today, design education in most fields does not include this master-apprentice relationship. As formal design education moved into colleges and universities, professional identity cultivation was based on theory development and learning-by-doing academic experiences. Formal education cannot replace the master, but you can. By engaging in this journey, you can become a master in cultivating your designer professional identity.

You Are Now a Member

Welcome to the ever-changing design professional community! While our profession is exciting, we are still in the process of cultivating and discovering a professional identity. Think about the word *design*. It invokes images of dynamic creativity, flexibility, and innovation. In a multidisciplinary community such as *design*, neither the profession nor its professional identity is stagnant (Ahlgren & Tett, 2010; Baumeister & Muraven, 1996). As a member of the *design* community, your professional identity plays an important role in your education, professional development, and career progression. Your journey does not have a deadline. Your professional identity will continue to develop until you breathe your last breath, long after your formal education is complete. Your journey is not down a straight and narrow highway. You will exit here to gain a new perspective and exit there to find a new approach to a seemingly old design situation. With every exit, there is an onramp back to the highway as you continue to strengthen your designer professional identity. A weak professional identity has a direct influence on the quality of your work and affects the image of *design* as a profession (Murphy et al., 2015; Woo, 2013), while a strong professional identity secures your membership in the *design* community while essential for the *design* profession to flourish (Norlyk, 2016).

Your Professional Identity Journey Begins Here

Your journey in developing a professional identity will include an understanding of your role and responsibilities while experiencing a sense of satisfaction and pride in the *design* field (Patall et al., 2014; Skorikov &

Vondracek, 2011). Your self-understanding as a professional, fundamental aspects of professionalism (Marquardt et al., 2016), performance (Adams et al., 2011), career decisions (Lichtenstein et al., 2009), and psychological wellbeing (Sharma & Sharma, 2010) will grow and be transformed as your professional identity journey evolves. To begin this journey, however, you need a map.

Your Journey Map

This book is your journey map where you will discover how to cultivate your designer professional identity. The goal of this book is to help you develop your self-perception and self-identification, and understandings you will draw upon to construct your professional identity (Williams, 2013). Each segment will focus on a different skill of professional identity. The segment will include a definition, research on the skill, and its alignment with professional identity development. You will learn how to cultivate this skill with specific activities that will then support your professional identity development. One final note, this book is not meant to be a step-by-step process, but rather your guide. Each segment provides elements to establish designer professional identity that you can work on individually and iteratively. You will most likely revisit the segments numerous times over your career, gaining new insight with each visit. This is your personal journey, so begin by looking at all the segments then decide where you want your journey to begin.

Before you begin, you will want to prepare yourself to get the most out of your journey. This includes an understanding of the definition of professional identity and how professional identity impacts you as a designer. Let's begin by looking at what professional identity is.

What Is Professional Identity?

It is human nature to want to belong to a community, with a group of friends, and in your profession. Professional identity is the sense of belonging to a group and, so, to a profession. It is a dynamic understanding of professional responsibilities, actions, beliefs, and values. This dynamic process of social- and self-understanding as a professional develops over time and is reshaped based on your mindset and your role and responsibilities. The professional identity development process involves being consciously aware as a designer. Both social and self-perception play an important role in your professional identity development (Skorikov & Vondracek, 2011) as it is affected by social, demographic, and personality factors (Crossley & Vivekananda-Schmidt, 2009). Let's take a look at professional identity and you.

How Does Professional Identity Relate to Me?

On an individual level, professional identity is a state of mind or a level of awareness that allows you to identify with a specific group or profession (Kunrath et al., 2016). Your designer professional identity started during your professional education and continues throughout your practice as a designer (Godsey, 2011). Reflect on a moment you may have had so far in your educational journey. Was there an article you read, an assignment you completed or a class discussion you participated in where you thought "this is for me!" You may not have known what it was that was exactly for you, or did not have the answers, but something clicked where you thought, "I want to know more." This was your professional identity emerging. This is what your professional identity looks like. Your personal traits such as your empathy, ability to collaborate, make decisions, reflect, deal with uncertainty, your ethics, creativity, communication or social abilities, and responsibility to continue to learn are characteristics of your professional identity. These characteristics influence and promote the growth of your competencies and the development of your personal self-understanding as a professional. Furthermore, social context or interactions between you and others contribute to the development of a range of self-understanding that you can draw from in the process of constructing a professional identity (Williams, 2013). An understanding of the importance and construction of belongingness through learning and skill development also connects you to your professional identity (Baumeister & Leary, 1995). As you can see, identity is neither stable, nor a final achievement; it is a never-ending process (Dent & Whitehead, 2001) that includes the blending of personal and professional attributes. Developing your designer professional identity is a psychological process of identification and involves self-perception and social perception of your designer professionalism. This life-long learning process requires the integration of your personal values, morals, and skills with the norms of the design profession.

How Does Professional Identity Relate to Me as a Designer?

As a designer, your professional identity development began during your higher education experience and becomes especially relevant in your transition from student to professional (Trede & McEwen, 2012). Reflect on where you are right now in your career development. Are you in the early stages of your career, mid-career, or moving to a new career? Wherever you are at this moment, you are making a commitment to the design profession. This commitment is also a commitment to your professional identity development. For a designer, professional identity is different from other professions because it involves how designers know, think, or work but we cannot see thinking; we can see practices and activities (Friedman, 2000). Those new to design face many difficulties in adapting to a work environment and the complexities of the field (Evetts, 2003; Tracey & Hutchinson, 2013). Your professional identity as a designer also differs from other professions due to the uncertainties relating to the boundaries of professional activities (Tracey & Hutchinson, 2016). As a designer, you may create physical products, solve organizational and/or societal problems, or focus on service and/or on experience design. You will need to incorporate knowledge of political issues and business methods, operations and marketing, and understand business and technology. As a designer, you will work across disciplines so it is crucial that you understand human beings, but in order to do that, you must first understand yourself. You must be educated and knowledgeable in your design area while being grounded in your belongingness to the design community; all this is possible with a developed professional identity. So now that you have a better understanding of what professional identity is and how it relates to being a designer, it is time for you to begin your journey. Each segment is its own exit on your designer professional identity highway, so skim through the book and choose a segment that you would like to delve into first. Enjoy your journey!

Takeaways: Your Professional Identity Journey Begins Here

- Your professional identity plays an important role in your education, professional development, and career progression.
- Your professional identity is your personal journey.
- Your professional identity is a wonderful never-ending process.
- Your professional identity requires that you understand human beings, starting with yourself.

Cultivating Your Professional Identity Reflections

1. **The beginning**: Reflect on the moment when your professional identity began to emerge. When was it? Where were you? How did it make you feel? How did you feel about those around you?
2. **Can I design**: Makayla questions herself, "Can I design?" How about you? Why?

> *It is not easy to explain to people what it is to be a designer. They... seem to think that you are either a vague arty-type or a hard-nosed technologist...your 'softer' audience will tend to assume you are a technofreak, and the technologists will think that you spend your days painting flowers on coffee machines.*
>
> (Dorst, 2003, p. 14)

References

Adams, R. S., Daly, S. R., Mann, L. M., & Dall'Alba, G. (2011). Being a professional: Three lenses into design thinking, acting, and being. *Design Studies*, *32*(6), 588–607. doi: https://doi.org/10.1016/j.destud.2011.07.004

Ahlgren, L., & Tett, L. (2010). Work-based learning, identity and organisational culture. *Studies in Continuing Education*, *32*(1), 17–27. doi: https://doi.org/10.1080/01580370903534280

Baumeister, R. F., & Leary, M. R. (1995). The need to belong: Desire for interpersonal attachments as a fundamental human motivation. *Psychological Bulletin*, *117*(3), 497–529. doi: https://doi.org/10.1037/0033-2909.117.3.497

Baumeister, R. F., & Muraven, M. (1996). Identity as adaptation to social, cultural, and historical context. *Journal of Adolescence*, *19*(5), 405–416. doi: https://doi.org/10.1006/jado.1996.0039

Crossley, J., & Vivekananda-Schmidt, P. (2009). The development and evaluation of a Professional Self Identity Questionnaire to measure evolving Professional

Self-Identity in health and social care students. *Medical Teacher, 31*(12), 603–607. doi: https://doi.org/10.3109/01421590903193547

Dent, M., & Whitehead, S. (2001). Configuring the 'new' professional. In M. Dent & S. Whitehead (Eds.), *Managing professional identities: Knowledge, performativities and the "new" professional* (1st ed., pp. 1–16). Routledge.

Dorst, K. (2003). *Understanding design: 150 reflections on being a designer*. Bis Publishers.

Evetts, J. (2003). The sociological analysis of professionalism: Occupational change in the modern world. *International Sociology, 18*(2), 395–415. doi: https://doi.org/10.1177/0268580903018002005

Friedman, K. (2000). Design knowledge: Context, content and continuity. In D. Durling, & K. Friedman (Ed.), *Doctoral education in design: Foundations for the future* (pp. 5–16). Staffordshire University Press.

Godsey, S. R. (2011). *Student perceptions of professional identity and cultural competence* (Publication No. 3457068) [Doctoral dissertations, University of Minnesota]. ProQuest LLC.

Kunrath, K., Cash, P., & Li-Ying, J. (2016). Designer's identity: Personal attributes and design skills. Proceedings of International Design Conference, 1729–1740. https://www.designsociety.org/download-publication/38983/DESIGNER'S+IDENTI-TY:+PERSONAL+ATTRIBUTES+AND+DESIGN+SKILLS

Lichtenstein, G., Loshbaugh, H. G., Claar, B., Chen, H. L., Jackson, K., & Sheppard, S. D. (2009). An engineering major does not (necessarily) an engineer make: Career decision making among undergraduate engineering majors. *Journal of Engineering Education, 98*(3), 227–234. doi: https://doi.org/10.1002/j.2168-9830.2009.tb01021.x

Marquardt, M. K., Gantman, A. P., Gollwitzer, P. M., & Oettingen, G. (2016). Incomplete professional identity goals override moral concerns. *Journal of Experimental Social Psychology, 65*, 31–41. doi: https://doi.org/10.1016/j.jesp.2016.03.001

Murphy, M., Chance, S., & Conlon, E. (2015). Designing the identities of engineers. In S. H. Christensen, C. Didier, A. Jamison, M. Meganck, C. Mitcham, & B. Newberry (Eds.), *Engineering identities, epistemologies and values. Philosophy of engineering and technology* (pp. 41–64). Springer. doi: https://doi.org/10.1007/978-3-319-16172-3_3

Norlyk, B. (2016). Professional discourse and professional identities at cross-purposes: Designer or entrepreneur? *Globe: A Journal of Language, Culture and Communication, 3*, 96–107. doi: https://doi.org/10.5278/ojs.globe.v3i0.1244

Patall, E. A., Sylvester, B. J., & Han, C. woo. (2014). The role of competence in the effects of choice on motivation. *Journal of Experimental Social Psychology, 50*, 27–44. doi: https://doi.org/10.1016/j.jesp.2013.09.002

Sharma, S., & Sharma, M. (2010). Self, social identity and psychological well-being. *Psychological Studies, 55*(2), 118–136. doi: https://doi.org/10.1007/s12646-010-0011-8

Skorikov, V. B., & Vondracek, F. W. (2011). Occupational identity. In S. J. Schwartz, K. Luyckx, & V. L. Vignoles (Eds.), *Handbook of identity theory and research* (pp. 693–714). Springer. doi: https://doi.org/10.1007/978-1-4419-7988-9_29

Tracey, M. W., & Hutchinson, A. (2013). Developing designer identity through reflection. *Educational Technology, 53*(3), 28–32. https://digitalcommons.wayne.edu/coe_aos/6/

Tracey, M. W., & Hutchinson, A. (2016). Uncertainty, reflection, and designer identity development. *Design Studies, 42*, 86–109. doi: https://doi.org/10.1016/j.destud.2015.10.004

Trede, F., & McEwen, C. (2012). Developing a critical professional identity. In J. Higgs, R. Barnett, S. Billett, M. Hutchings, & F. Trede (Eds.), *Practice-based education.*

Perspectives and strategies (3rd ed., pp. 27–40). Sense Publishers. doi: https://doi.org/10.1007/978-94-6209-128-3_3

Williams, J. (2013). *Constructing new professional identities*. Sense Publishers. doi: https://doi.org/10.1007/978-94-6209-260-0

Woo, H. R. (2013). *Instrument construction and initial validation: Professional Identity Scale in Counseling (PISC)* (Publication No. 3566722) [Doctoral dissertation, The University of Iowa]. ProQuest LLC.

EMPATHY

Makayla was working at the kitchen table watching her husband Tyler trying to teach their 7-year-old daughter Kassandra addition facts. Their older daughter, Jayla, was a brilliant student in math, and Tyler could not understand why Kassandra could not learn the way Jayla did. Kassandra was crying, Tyler was yelling, and no one was learning addition. Makayla could feel his frustration, and when she looked at Kassandra, she felt extreme sorrow for this child who already had an aversion to school. She could see the fear in Kassandra's eyes because she could not grasp what her dad was trying to teach her. Makayla felt helpless. "I should be able to design a way for Kassandra to learn addition facts that works for her" she thought. "What do I need to do to help Kassandra learn?"

Empathy is the ability to stand in someone else's place while standing in your own.

Welcome to empathy. Fold your journey map to this stop and get ready to embrace empathy and empathic design. One of the best things about being a designer is your design can have an impact on a person's life. Design is a human endeavor, so you need to have empathy, for your audience and their needs, for others involved in the design project, and for yourself as you attempt to tackle wicked design problems. So, take a deep breath as it is time to explore empathy, what it is, and how to engage in it. And so, we begin our empathy journey.

What Is Empathy?

Have you ever played the shadow game as a child? Outside when the sun is shining, you run to stand in someone else's shadow. While standing in their shadow, you are still standing in your own. This is what empathy looks like. Empathy is not sympathy. When asking terminal cancer patients receiving palliative care about their experiences with sympathy and empathy, they explained that sympathy was perceived as self-serving while empathy was perceived as genuine (Sinclair et al., 2017). Empathy is not self-serving. In design, it is the ability to "be" as the other, while remaining your whole self, or the ability to stand in someone else's shadow while standing in your own. Makayla experienced empathy for Tyler trying to teach addition facts, for Kassandra, afraid she would never learn addition facts, while feeling empathy for herself in her inability to help them. Empathy in design is influenced by your ability and willingness to develop deliverables that meet your audience of focus' needs (Kouprie & Visser, 2009). Empathy drives design as a means to an end. The end is a meaningful design deliverable that meets your audience's immediate needs. Where does empathy come from?

You were born with the capacity for empathy, but it is learned behavior that grows over time from self-awareness. The more you become aware of your emotions, the more you are able to recognize the emotions in others. Your empathy is one element of your professional identity development (Walther et al., 2017). When you have empathy in design, you have a heightened understanding of your audience, allowing you to step away from designing for yourself and step toward designing for them (Levy, 2018). Empathy drives action in design.

What Is Empathic Design?

In 1990, Sam Farber watched his beloved wife Betsey struggling to hold her potato peeler due to arthritis. "Why do ordinary kitchen tools have to hurt your hands?" he thought. He promised he would make Betsey a better peeler. The result is OXO, a worldwide company with the goal of designing thoughtful cooking tools. Farber is an empathic designer. Empathic design is an important tool to have in your designer toolbox. It does not replace design, rather it enhances design as it seeks to get closer to the lives and experiences of your audience (Baaki & Tracey, 2019). When you employ empathic design, you will call on your observational skills to learn about your audience and their context as part of the design process with the goal of understanding their experience. Every design decision you make will be made with your audience in the forefront throughout the entire design process. You will reflect, interact, and act on your audience's behavior during design. Embracing empathic design allows you to develop products that are both innovative and responsive to your actual users' needs and desires (Battarbee et al., 2015). It increases your sensitivity to your audience as well as to your design potential. Your ultimate goal as a designer is to engage in empathy and empathic design to create a meaningful design, resulting in a deliverable that answers your audiences' needs.

How Do I Design with Empathy?

Roger Ebert, a well-known movie critic commenting on empathy in film, reflected that "the movies are like a machine that generates empathy. It lets you understand a little bit more about different hopes, aspirations, dreams, and fears. It helps us to identify with the people who are sharing this journey with us."

You are on a journey to design with empathy. This, however, does not simply mean having empathy for your audience. Designing with empathy also involves having empathy for you as the designer, as well as for the localized context of use (Baaki & Tracey, 2019). When designing with empathy, you create a meaningful design deliverable for what your audience needs in their specific situation. Think back to Farber's design of the potato peeler, although used by many, he designed it with the specific purpose of aiding his arthritic wife peel potatoes. There are two sides to a localized context of use. The first side is where you reflect on and have empathy for your audience, others involved in the design, and for you in the design context. The other side of the localized context of use is action. You will then act. As a designer, the key to empathic design is to act on that localized context of use through introspection, interaction, and intention (Herman et al., 2022).

Empathy for Your Audience

When engaging in empathy and empathic design, you make decisions while keeping in mind your audience and their context. When you look deeply at who your audience is, you open yourself up in a responsive way to their lives, their feelings, and their experiences. By having empathic feelings for others, you will become motivated to address their needs (Batson, 2009).

D. Kirk Hamilton, a professor of Architecture at Texas A&M University, wrote an editorial on design for an evolving patient experience (Hamilton, 2022). When addressing hospital patient care, he painted a picture of the patient, identifying categories that might contribute to their experience. Hamilton urged designers to look at the lived experience of a patient including their daily activities, the routines of caregiving, toileting, food, entertainment, education, rest interruptions, noise, and sleep. He maintained that any or all of these may impact the patient's perception of their overall experience. Although designing for each individual patient experience might be challenging, Hamilton wondered at what point is standardization too simplistic and ineffective for varied usage (Hamilton, 2022). When you think about your audience, do you think about them as deeply and wholly as Hamilton? Do you take a deep dive into reflecting on how they will experience your design?

A design team engaged in empathy when they visualized their audience interacting with an activity they were designing. The team reflected and discussed how the audience would feel during the activity (Tracey & Hutchinson, 2019). They asked each other: Is the audience in a place to engage in this activity? Are they prepared physically, emotionally, and cognitively? How will the audience feel engaged in the activity? What will the audiences' outcome be after the activity? The design team visualized the audience before, during, and after the activity, in both their cognitive and emotional states, and designed appropriately. The outcome the designers envisioned for the audience experience matched the audience's perceptions of their experience during the activity. In other words, the design team engaged in empathy for the audience's experience during the activity. The audience's experience with the activity aligned with how the designers perceived it would be. Engaging in empathy for your audience includes stepping into their shoes while staying in your own.

Empathy for You

Ann was hired to design an intervention to help prepare adults to take their high school equivalency exam. She immediately experienced empathy for her audience as she was the first in her family to go to college. Ann dropped out before completing her degree due to drowning student loan debt and having to constantly defend her decision to study design to family and friends. Twenty years later, she went back to school, completing her undergraduate and graduate degrees in three years. Today, she embraced this design challenge as she not only remembered her educational journey but also reflected on her family members, some of whom were able to obtain their high school equivalency and others who could not. Ann's past experiences, life events, and design knowledge serve her well as she designs for her audience. Her precedents and empathy for herself and her audience bring her closer to the design of a successful deliverable (Baaki & Tracey, 2019).

You are an integral part of the design process bringing your biases, inspirations, and uncertainty to each design (Tracey & Hutchinson, 2018). You also use your knowledge, experience, and intuition to make design decisions while creating deliverables (Tracey, 2015). There is so much of you, including your emotions, in every design you complete although it may be difficult for you to identify how your emotions are affecting your design decisions. In empathy, the more you become aware of your emotions, the more you are able to recognize the emotions in others. Like Ann, having empathy for you as a designer means recognizing the emotions, experiences, interests, and biases you bring to the design.

In the past, designers were actually encouraged to avoid inserting their judgments, experiences, or values in their designs. We now know that it is important for you as a designer to establish your designer precedents, which are memories of existing designs, life experiences, and other influences that help mold you into the designer you are (Tracey et al., 2014). Precedent is a key form of design knowledge; it is the knowledge you obtain from any life experience that supports future design decisions. As you move through design, you will rely on design intelligence, precedents, and intuition in order to create meaningful deliverables (Tracey & Hutchinson, 2013).

How do designer precedents relate to empathy for you? You bring your precedents including your interests, biases, and understandings (Cross, 2011) to every design you engage in. Empathy for yourself as a designer includes accepting what you personally bring to the design (precedents) and how it influences the design. You may be uncomfortable admitting how your biases, understandings, or lack of understandings impact the design, so it is important for you to acknowledge your precedents and have empathy for yourself as you grapple with design decisions and the final deliverable.

Empathy for the Localized Context of Use

A design team working with an organization specializing in group homes for adults with developmental disabilities designed a staff instructional intervention on group home communication. The executive team stressed the need for the design to be individualized, online, and short, as group home staff do not have time during the day for extensive learning. The design team created an interactive short instructional intervention applying all of the content and requirements the executive team requested. The executive team was thrilled with the product. Six months later, when the COVID-19 outbreak resulted in the executive team members being forced to cover sick direct care workers' shifts, the executives realized the lack of communication could not be resolved with the instructional intervention as designed. Communication regarding the residents' medications, house make-up, staff needs, etc., needed to be specific to each house, something they had not thought of. The organization facilitates 12 group homes of varying sizes. In some cases, the group home is small and requires only one direct care worker per shift whereas at larger group homes, there are multiple direct care workers per shift. The executive team needed a design for a localized context of use, one for each of the 12 homes that met each home's direct care workers' immediate shift needs. A localized context of use emphasizes specific moments where context is scaled back to what is needed in a situation (Baaki & Tracey, 2019).

When engaging in empathy with your audience, you need to imagine other (Batson, 2009), which allows you to remain a designer while opening yourself to the feelings and experiences of the audience. These feelings and experiences include not only what the audience brings to the environment, but how they interact with the design. In other words, what is needed in this product for this audience at this moment. This is designing for a localized context of use. This approach (Baaki & Tracey, 2019) pushes you out of the realm of theoretical interventions into intentional action steps. It forces you to focus on a narrow scope in terms of context (time/space), in terms of context of use (time/space and audience), and in terms of context of use approach (time/space, audience, and design team intentions) (Herman et al., 2022). Empathic design suggests that it is not enough to try and imagine the feelings of your end user (Dandavate et al., 1996). You must then engage in introspection, interaction, and intention (Thomas et al., 2002) while reflecting on your own contexts and those of the given circumstances. And then you must embrace design action (Herman et al., 2022).

Find a fallen tree or an old stump, sit down, and take a quick break. Take out your map and notice that one of your segment destinations is Diversity, Equity, and Inclusion. In that segment, we spend a lot of time on introspection, interaction, and intention which we call the 3 Is. After you complete empathy, you may want to visit the Diversity, Equity, and Inclusion segment. While you are here at empathy, let's overview the 3 Is.

> **Introspection.** Engaging in introspection begins when you empathically examine the context surrounding the specific moment of the intervention. You narrow the focus to a design for that specific moment of use, which allows you to identify the critical forces at work that can affect the understanding

and use of the deliverable (Meloncon, 2017). You must put in the work to educate yourself, connect, and communicate with your audience on a deep and personal level, and determine the best approach to move forward.

Interaction. Beyond collaborative introspection with peers, interacting with your audience of use includes a co-determination of specific use cases. When you consider a specific moment of use, you reflect and design with empathy on how your audience will use your design and the numerous ways your audience may then act. The moment of use may be a short moment (communicating group home resident's daily medication needs) or a longer moment (an organizational communication process to align resident care).

Intention. The intention of your design must be to act with empathy. You will fail unless you take action. Taking action means determining the specific moment of use for your design and designing for that moment. Designing for a specific action case makes a design tangible instead of theoretical.

Through empathy, you get closer to the lives and experiences of your audience in an effort to increase the likelihood that your design will meet their needs (Kouprie & Visser, 2009). Empathy in design is central to problem-solving, human-centered design, and design thinking (Bohorquez, 2019). You are required to have a deep understanding of people to create meaningful products, services, and experiences (Bohorquez, 2019). Your empathy also supports your ability to visualize the possibilities of the design by envisioning your audience's experience.

How Do I Cultivate My Designer Empathy?

By championing, nurturing, and practicing empathy regularly, you will cultivate your designer professional identity. Fostering your designer empathy includes reflecting on three layers of empathy in design: (1) empathy toward humans, (2) empathy toward design, and (3) empathy toward techniques (Mattelmäki et al., 2014). As we take a deeper dive into each of these, reflect on how you can apply these layers to cultivate your designer identity.

Empathy Toward Humans

Throughout this segment, we have talked about developing empathy for your audience, yourself, and the context you are designing for. Empathy begins with human interaction. As an empathic designer, you will consistently gather inspiration and information about your audience, their experiences, and their contexts. One way to do this is through *Progressive Discovery* (Battarbee et al., 2015). If it is difficult for you to identify with your audience, perhaps their culture and values are fundamentally different than your own; you can gain empathy one step at a time, through a progressive journey of empathy, growing, and learning. Begin your journey by creating audience profiles through information and data gathering. You may interview, observe, and ask questions to the individuals you will be designing for. This is only the beginning of your *Progressive Discovery* journey, however. Take this a step further by interviewing others in your audience's world. It may be coworkers, customers, and/or supervisors. What are their stories? What are they telling you and each other? As you gain the perspective of people who interact with your audience, you will learn more about how they interact in their world. The final step on your journey of *Progressive Discovery* is to live in their shoes while still maintaining your designer identity. Allow yourself at least one morning or afternoon to do the work they do; interact with the people they interact with and live the life they live. This will help you rethink your initial assumptions and increase your empathy for your audience.

Empathy Toward Design

Empathy is central to problem-solving in design. It is also vital to the design process. Empathy enables you to appreciate people's realities and perspectives. It helps you uncover insights and develop solutions based on people's experiences and behavior. When you have empathy toward design, you seek out potential design directions and solutions (Bohorquez, 2019). One strategy to promote empathy toward design is the *Enhanced Design Brief.*

Used as a mechanism to establish the conditions of the project, the design brief has been a standard practice in design. The standard brief includes a description of the problem, it may provide an explanation on how to solve the problem and the steps that will be taken. The *Enhanced Design Brief* shifts the focus solely on the problem and pushes designers to consider the audience's experiences and concerns. By framing the design problem in the localized context of use for the audience of focus, you increase the chances of focusing on the audience's challenges, their needs, and their context. In the *Enhanced Design Brief*, you provide detailed plans of the research and data gathering activities you will use to explore and understand the experience of your audience and your stakeholders. These activities may include interviews, observations, storytelling, and visuals. The final key point to the *Enhanced Design Brief* is that it is iterative. It is not done once in the beginning of the design project, but is revisited numerous times over the lifetime of the project. This will promote many more interactions between you, your audience, and your stakeholders.

Empathy Toward Techniques

There are numerous design techniques that can increase your empathy in design. By creating personas, prototypes, and visualization tools to communicate and explore the design problem and your audience, you can engage in empathy toward your design team, your audience of focus, and your stakeholders. The *Dialogue and Critique* technique can raise awareness regarding audience-related issues while promoting empathy in you and your design team. Begin by identifying your audience and stakeholders involved in the design problem. Engage in dialogue with your audience of focus, stakeholders, and your design team to specifically gather all their different perspectives as it relates to the design problem. Gather information by using techniques such as a "day in the life" to better understand your audience's needs. When you have gathered your data, it is time for the design team to conduct a *Dialogue and Critique* session. Dedicate at least two hours, one hour to dialogue and one hour to critique. In the first hour, through displaying empathic behaviors, discuss your understanding of the audience, the stakeholders, and their needs. Maintain the focus on user-related issues. Remember that this is dialogue, no decisions are to be made, just deep empathic discussion. At the end of the hour of discussion, brainstorm and document the preferred course of action for the design.

In the second hour, you conduct the critique. The team looks at the possible design action to determine if they address the human experience of your audience. Rather than focusing on creating your product, focus on the experience. Does your design improve and enrich your audience's life? The goal of the critique is to maintain the focus on your audience and their physical, emotional, and social interactions with your design in their context of use.

Takeaways: Empathy

- When you engage in empathy during design, you step away from designing for you and step toward designing for your audience.
- When you engage in empathy and empathic design, you create a meaningful design, resulting in a deliverable that meets your audience's localized context of use.
- When you engage in empathy and empathic design, you make decisions while keeping in mind your audience, you, and their context.
- You act on your empathic design through introspection, interaction, and intention.

Exercises to Develop Your Designer Empathy

1. **Two sides of the same coin**: Reflect on and write a detailed idea that you truly believe in. It could be something small or large, such as personal recycling or global warming. Immediately after completing your idea, defend the opposite side of that idea. You can do this alone or with another person or group of people. The goal is to put yourself in the shoes of someone having the opposing view.
2. **Empathy in action, the 3 Is**: Engaging in design through introspection, interaction, and intention can help you design for a localized context of use. Read this scenario and reflect on the questions below:
   - Norfolk Public Safety (NPS) is reevaluating its safety and security procedures for its 9-1-1 dispatchers. NPS has asked you to develop 9-1-1 dispatcher training for new dispatchers. You are focusing on one training segment: Assisting callers. Specifically, 9-1-1 dispatchers must be able to guide a caller,

over the phone, on how to perform CPR until help arrives. Open yourself in a responsive way to your audience of focus – new 9-1-1 dispatchers.

- Reflect on and describe the context surrounding the specific moment of the intervention?
- How would you interact with your audience of focus, stakeholders, etc., to gather the information you would need for this design?
- How would you design the dispatcher training for the moment of use?

Exercise for Those Who Teach Others

1. The Power of Observation

The purpose of this activity is for your students to experience the challenges and benefits of direct observation. Over the next week have them do the following:

- Think of something you do on a regular basis that you can observe others doing (e.g., ordering a coffee at a local coffee shop).
- Go to the place where you do this (e.g., your local Starbucks).
- Sit for 60 minutes and observe others performing the task you do (e.g., ordering coffee).
- Observe the people's actions, the environment they are in (their own personal environment and the larger environmental space), the interactions they have with others and with objects, and who they are.
- Observe how individuals do it differently from how you do it (e.g., pay cash instead of using their phone)
- What do you want to know about them? For example, why did they use cash?
- Open yourself in a responsive way while observing them by tapping into your sight, touch, smell, and hearing. For example, why do you think she used cash? What do you observe to help you answer your questions? Write it down.

- Observe yourself during this activity. Be mindful of your own personal reactions and as you observe others write it down. Are you bored? Excited? Angry? Impatient? Why?
- What details did you notice watching someone else perform a task that you have performed many times yourself?
- How did you think your own experience colored your observations?
- Spend 60 minutes observing others and yourself and document whatever you feel, see, hear, touch, and smell.

     Have them present what they observed in whatever manner they would like to do Would they want to tell a story, show visuals, bring something for the class to see, smell, touch, and/or hear? Make sure you allow each student 10 minutes or so to present their findings.

(Adapted from Neck et al., 2014)

Energy for Your Journey

The processes whereby one person can come to know the internal state of another and can be motivated to respond with sensitive care are of enormous importance for our life together.

(Batson, 2009, p. 11)

References

Baaki, J., & Tracey, M. W. (2019). Weaving a localized context of use: What it means for instructional design. *Journal of Applied Instructional Design, 8*(1), 2–13. https://253f0a53-bb62-46af-b495-b4548f4d5d90.filesusr.com/ugd/c9b0ce_d055972f6f-b942098860aac6071cc11e.pdf

Batson, C. D. (2009). These things called empathy: Eight related by distinct phenomena. In J. Decety & W. Ickes (Eds.), *The social neuroscience of empathy* (pp. 2–15). MIT Press. doi: https://doi.org/10.7551/mitpress/9780262012973.003.0002

Battarbee, K., Suri, J. F., & Howard, S. G. (2015). Empathy on the edge: Scaling and sustaining a human-centred approach to innovation. *Harvard Business Review*, Winter 2015, 61–65.

Bohorquez, F. A. T. (2019). Developing empathy in the academic design studio: Conclusions from an empirical study in graduate and undergraduate programs in industrial design. *Diseño y Creación Foro Académico Internacional*, 281–289. http://hdl.handle.net/20.500.12010/8608

Cross, N. (2011). *Design thinking: Understanding how designers think and work*. Berg.

Dandavate, U., Sanders, E. B.-N., & Stuart, S. (1996). Emotions matter: User empathy in the product development process. *Proceedings of the Human Factors and Ergonomics Society Annual Meeting, 40*(7), 415–418. doi: https://doi.org/10.1177/154193129604000709

Hamilton, D. K. (2022). Design for an evolving patient experience. *HERD: Health Environments Research & Design Journal, 15*(1), 22–28. doi: https://doi.org/10.1177/19375867211060826

Herman, K., Baaki, J., & Tracey, M. W. (2022). "Faced with given circumstances": A localized context of use approach. In B. Hokanson, M. Exter, M. Schmidt, & A. Tawfik (Eds.), *Toward inclusive learning design: Social justice, equity, and community*. Springer.

Kouprie, M., & Visser, F. S. (2009). A framework for empathy in design: Stepping into and out of the user's life. *Journal of Engineering Design, 20*(5), 437–448. doi: https://doi.org/10.1080/09544820902875033

Levy, M. (2018). Educating for empathy in software engineering course. REFSQ Workshops. http://ceur-ws.org/Vol-2075/FIRE18_paper2.pdf

Mattelmäki, T., Vaajakallio, K., & Koskinen, I. (2014). What happened to empathic design? *Design Issues, 30*(1), 67–77. doi: https://doi.org/10.1162/DESI_a_00249

Meloncon, L. K. (2017). Patient experience design: Expanding usability methodologies for healthcare. *Communication Design Quarterly, 5*(2), 19–28. doi: https://doi.org/10.1145/3131201.3131203.

Neck, H. M., Greene, P. G., & Brush, C. G. (2014). *Teaching entrepreneurship: A practice-based approach*. Edgar Elgar Publishing Limited.

Sinclair, S., Beamer, K., Hack, T. F., McClement, S., Raffin Bouchal, S., Chochinov, H. M., & Hagen, N. A. (2017). Sympathy, empathy, and compassion: A grounded theory study of palliative care patients' understandings, experiences, and preferences. *Palliative Medicine, 31*(5), 437–447. doi: https://doi.org/10.1177/0269216316663499

Thomas, M., Mitchell, M., & Joseph, R. (2002). The third dimension of ADDIE: A cultural embrace. *TechTrends, 46*(2), 40–45. http://link.springer.com/article/10.1007/BF02772075

Tracey, M. W. (2015). Design team collaboration with a complex design problem. In Brad Hokanson, G. Clinton, & M. W. Tracey (Eds.), *The design of learning experience. Educational communications and technology: Issues and innovations* (pp. 93–108). Springer. doi: https://doi.org/10.1007/978-3-319-16504-2_7

Tracey, M. W., & Hutchinson, A. (2013). Developing designer identity through reflection. *Educational Technology, 53*(3), 28–32. https://digitalcommons.wayne.edu/coe_aos/6/

Tracey, M. W., & Hutchinson, A. (2018). Reflection and professional identity development in design education. *International Journal of Technology and Design Education, 28*(1), 263–285. doi: https://doi.org/10.1007/s10798-016-9380-1

Tracey, M. W., & Hutchinson, A. (2019). Empathic design: Imagining the cognitive and emotional learner experience. *Educational Technology Research and Development, 67*(5), 1259–1272. doi: https://doi.org/10.1007/s11423-019-09683-2

Tracey, M. W., Hutchinson, A., & Grzebyk, T. Q. (2014). Instructional designers as reflective practitioners: Developing professional identity through reflection. *Educational Technology Research and Development, 62*(3), 315–334. doi: https://doi.org/10.1007/s11423-014-9334-9

Walther, J., Miller, S. E., & Sochacka, N. W. (2017). A model of empathy in engineering as a core skill, practice orientation, and professional way of being. *Journal of Engineering Education, 106*(1), 123–148. doi: https://doi.org/10.1002/jee.20159

UNCERTAINTY

Makayla: Makayla's first project was to participate in a needs assessment for a pizza company. Uncertain how to set her boundaries for her design, she reached out via email to her senior design supervisor looking for any direction or clarification to unravel her uncertainty. The email response was simple: engage in your uncertainty. Upon reflection, she realized she needed to focus her initial needs assessment on one pizzeria instead of all eight restaurants in the pizzeria family. Once she realized this, she understood that she was engaging in uncertainty. In the moment (not looking back and not looking forward), she reflected "I am learning quickly – or not quickly enough – that I am overlooking things."

Design is about exploring the unknown requiring the designer to embrace uncertainty.

What Is Uncertainty in Design?

Welcome to uncertainty. Fold your journey map to this stop and get ready to accept and embrace uncertainty. As a designer, every design project you engage in will force you to learn something new. Like Makayla, in the beginning, you may have little understanding of the design problem or opportunity you are tasked to design an approach or intervention for, and you may feel uncertain. What is uncertainty? Uncertainty is a lack of adequate knowledge about events that may occur in the future or that may have already occurred but have not yet been revealed to you (Bar-Anan et al., 2009; Rosen et al., 2014). When we feel sure about a situation, we believe we can guess what will happen next, but when we feel uncertain about a situation, we may feel doubt when we anticipate what will happen next (Tracey & Hutchinson, 2018a). Most people experience uncertainty negatively, so they are motivated to reduce or eliminate it (Bar-Anan et al., 2009). You are not most people. You are a designer and as a designer, identifying, accepting, and ultimately embracing your uncertainty are important since design always involves new and novel challenges. In other words, uncertainty is natural in design. Although it may feel uncomfortable, the joy of designing lies in embracing uncertainty (Cross, 1982) and being comfortable with *not knowing* as you begin a new design journey. On this stop in your designer professional identity development journey, we are going to look at how to accept and ultimately embrace uncertainty and discover strategies to help you deal with your uncertainty during design.

How Does Openness Relate to Uncertainty?

Have you ever been completely open to a new situation or adventure? Ever taken a road trip with no end destination planned? When you are open, you can accept and embrace new experiences so as an open designer, you will welcome new and unusual ideas or approaches. Like embracing uncertainty, embracing openness is essential in developing your designer professional identity. If your professional identity includes the ability to be open, you will generally be flexible and ready for change. So, if you are open when you are feeling uncertain, you will be in a better position to be adaptable and enjoy the trip! Also, as an open designer, you tend to have greater resilience which helps you in uncertain situations (Bosma & Kunnen, 2001).

Openness or open-mindedness gives you the capacity to deal with uncertainty. We know that the level of openness you as a designer have, predicts how well you will do in radical innovation projects since it involves creative approaches to problems under conditions of high uncertainty. Design is a creative activity, and your openness becomes more important for more creative tasks (Reilly et al., 2002). Furthermore, if you are extremely open to new experiences, you most likely have a high level of curiosity and interest in getting others' ideas and insights (Wang & Noe, 2010). Openness and uncertainty go hand in hand in the development of your designer professional identity. The more open you are, the more you will be able to accept and embrace uncertainty in design.

How Do I Handle Uncertainty in Design?

Designing while embracing uncertainty can lead you to new possibilities and insights that can result in innovations (Chumakovaa & Kornilovb, 2013; Kornilova et al., 2018). Two of the ways you can handle uncertainty in design are first to become more comfortable with uncertainty, and second, to become more skilled at reducing uncertainty. The approach you take may depend on your current designer ability and/ or the context you are designing in (Dugas et al., 2005). For example, if you are new to design, it may be difficult for you to be comfortable with uncertainty so it might feel better if you try to learn as much as you can as quickly as you can about the design opportunity and the context you are designing, in an effort to reduce your uncertainty. One of the many challenges with this approach is that uncertainty promotes creativity in design so when you attempt to reduce your uncertainty, you may also tend to reduce your creativity and innovation. The higher your intolerance for uncertainty, the more your creativity is impeded (Kornilova et al., 2018).

Design requires you to be creative and to be able to make decisions. Creativity draws on both your thoughts and your emotions. Your tolerance or intolerance for uncertainty impacts your thoughts and emotions in terms of decision-making. When you are uncomfortable with uncertainty you will pay more attention on reducing your uncertainty (Dugas et al., 2005; Kornilova et al., 2018) and may make less wise decisions because of the importance you are placing on reducing those uncomfortable feelings (Kornilova et al., 2018). In other words, if you are uncomfortable with uncertainty, you will pay more attention to information that will reduce your discomfort level rather than the information needed to design a creative intervention. So, the key is to develop your designer professional identity which will give you a higher tolerance for uncertainty, which will ultimately promote your creativity.

Knowing that when you engage in design you must spend a significant amount of time in a state of uncertainty, take a moment now to reflect on how you currently respond to uncertainty. How do you respond once you have entered an uncertain state? What is your current tolerance/intolerance for uncertainty? How does uncertainty influence how you currently think, feel, and act as a designer? While uncertainty from a specific situation, such as a new design project with all its unknowns, is associated with increased stress and intensified emotional reactions (Bar-Anan et al., 2009; Rosen et al., 2014), the way you recognize and handle your uncertainty impacts how you design and what you design.

How Do I Design with Uncertainty?

As a designer, you are essential to the design process, and so are your openness and your uncertainty (Tracey & Hutchinson, 2018a). When you begin a design project, you will quickly become aware of what it is that you know and don't know, so you will experience uncertainty very early in your design process. That uncertainty, called epistemic uncertainty, or uncertainty about what we know can actually motivate you toward solving the design problem through action (Ball et al., 2010). The more you attempt to learn about the design problem and create initial interventions, the more insight you will gain in the original design problem (Dorst & Cross, 2001) which will reduce your uncertainty. In other words, your uncertainty will actually help you learn about and solve the design problem!

Epistemic uncertainty or uncertainty about what we know is only one type of uncertainty. Design is also about innovation, and there are three other types of uncertainty that relate to innovation

(Lane & Maxfield, 2005). The first is called truth uncertainty, or whether what you think is true. If you are experiencing truth uncertainty, you might ask yourself "Is this truly the design problem?" or "How do I know this information is correct?" The second is called semantic uncertainty where you may ask "What does this proposal mean?" Here you are looking particularly for what the proposal means for all the people involved including the audience of focus, the stakeholders, and the design team. Do they all have the same understanding of the meaning of the proposal? What happens if they don't?

The third is called ontological uncertainty or uncertainty of the unknown, characterized by lack of knowledge about relevant items in a design problem or opportunity. This is the most personal and challenging form of uncertainty for you as a designer. It is this type of uncertainty, you will experience the most when designing because it involves looking at what you know and don't know about the elements in the design process, how they interact with each other, and the resulting changes to the elements due to these interactions. Both truth and semantic uncertainty are part of epistemic uncertainty, each somewhat manageable for you as a designer because they allow you to make predictions. Ontological uncertainty is the uncertainty in design that involves a higher level of complexity because you are dealing with your own lack of knowledge as well as unknown elements and interactions that may emerge, often in a rapidly changing situation. Ontological uncertainty also challenges your estimations of the future, since we cannot make predictions about elements that we are not aware of in the first place. This is the definition of uncertainty, the lack of adequate knowledge about events that may occur in the future! What you need to remember is that ontological uncertainty is the type of uncertainty that is most significant for innovation that results in change. The possibility for change in design hinges on how you as a designer can manage ontological uncertainty (Lane & Maxfield, 2005). You can now see how important it is to recognize your uncertainty and create ways to accept and embrace it as you engage in design.

Embracing uncertainty as a designer is so important, it is considered a "threshold concept," or one that holds the potential for new understandings that are necessary to move the design forward (Tovey et al., 2010).

Uncertainty as a "threshold concept" supports your transformative learning at both the personal and conceptual levels and provides you with an experience that is unforgettable, integrative, and inconvenient in a way that is motivating rather than limiting. Your tolerance for design uncertainty as a threshold concept emerges "the moment when a designer recognizes that the uncertainty present when approaching a design brief is *essential*, but at the same time *routine*, part of the design process" (Tovey et al., 2010, p. 6). Once you cross this threshold, the path can then be opened for you to examine how you personally navigate the uncertain design space in your individual design practice and in your way of being.

How Do I Cultivate My Designer Uncertainty?

Developing your designer uncertainty is essential to your emerging designer professional identity. Let's look at three specific design activities you can do to develop your designer uncertainty: (1) recognizing your uncertainty; (2) accepting uncertainty; (3) embracing uncertainty.

The first step in embracing your uncertainty in design is recognizing when and why you are uncertain. Designers deal with uncertainty in different ways. As we stated earlier, some try to reduce it while others embrace it during design. But before you can reduce or embrace your uncertainty you must recognize when you are uncertain. Recognizing your uncertainty during a design project begins when you take a few moments to check in with yourself and see where you are. There are two specific tools you can use to help you recognize your uncertainty, the first is practicing mindfulness and the second is engaging in reflective writing.

Mindfulness

Let's begin with mindfulness, which in its most basic form means paying full attention to something, in this case, your emotions and feelings. When you are being mindful you focus on being deeply aware of what you're sensing and feeling in the moment. You will need to slow down and really notice what you are doing and feeling. When you're mindful, you're taking your time to focus in a relaxed easy way. The three essential elements in practicing mindfulness are: (1) being aware; (2) being nonjudgmental; (3) being nonreactive. When you are engaged in these elements, you are maintaining a moment-by-moment awareness of your thoughts, feelings, bodily sensations, and surrounding environment through a self-compassionate lens. Here, you tune into what you are sensing in the present moment rather than the reworking the past or imagining the future. You can begin by simply reflecting on your current feelings and emotions. What it is you are feeling? How do you feel it physically, where in your body? What is causing you to feel this way? Mindfulness is not judgment, and it is important for you to be compassionate towards yourself and simply observe what you're thinking and feeling without judging those thoughts or feelings. Once you recognize that you are uncertain, you can decide how you want to handle that uncertainty. For you as a designer, mindfulness can foster creativity while working with uncertainty (Altay & Porter, 2021).

Reflection

The second tool to help you develop your designer professional identity with uncertainty is reflection, specifically reflective writing. By keeping a reflective journal, you can express your thoughts, emotions, wishes, and concerns about your design project. You can reflect on and write down all of the feelings of uncertainty you are experiencing. In design, reflection and reflective writing can help you take ownership of your learning process and become aware of your strengths and weaknesses (Gelmez & Bagli, 2018). Reflective writing of your thoughts and emotions also allows you to take a step back from them. When you have strong feelings of uncertainty, you may not be able to think of how to move your design forward, so taking a moment to reflectively write your thoughts and feelings down allows you to move one step away from the intense feelings that may be preventing you from designing.

Accepting

Once you recognize your feelings of uncertainty, the next step is accepting uncertainty as something in your life and in your design practice (Tracey & Hutchinson, 2018b). It is human nature to fight against what we're feeling if the feelings are uncomfortable, but when you experience feelings of uncertainty, remind yourself that your feelings are normal and an important part of the design process. There are two specific tools you can use to help you accept your uncertainty, the first is reflecting on past design experiences and the second is thoughtful internal dialogue.

Reflecting on Past Design Experiences

Let's begin by reflecting on past design experiences. In uncertain moments, we might feel stressed, stuck, or overwhelmed. Reflecting on past design experiences, both negative or difficult ones and positive or rewarding ones offer us growth opportunities. Reflecting on negative or difficult design experiences might seem hard to accept when we're going through them, but these moments are useful to look back and reflect on what we learned and how we can use that knowledge in the future. It is also rewarding to see that you made it through, that you succeeded in creating a finished design! Think about one or two design experiences from your past when you felt totally uncertain. Try to remember how that felt and the greatest challenges you faced because of the uncertainty. What did you do to handle it? Ask yourself, what did I learn about myself? What skills and strengths did I use in those design situations? Maybe you discovered you're resilient, you are persistent, or you discovered a way to use your uncertainty to creatively design. Whatever it was, by reflecting on past experiences both negative and positive you gain valuable insights and realize that although you were feeling uncertain during these designs, you lived through it and created completed design products! During these design experiences, you accepted uncertainty and were able to design through it and it is important for you to recognize those skills and abilities since they can support you in future uncertain situations. Reflecting on past design experiences while feeling current design uncertainty helps us accept the current feelings of uncertainty knowing we were there before, got through it, and learned from it!

Internal Dialogue

It's helpful to have habits and positive activities that can keep you grounded and give you a sense of relief. Thoughtful internal dialogue is an ongoing habit and activity you can engage in with yourself during moments of uncertainty. Thoughtful internal dialogue helps you reveal your thoughts, questions, beliefs, and ideas. When approached positively, thoughtful internal dialogue can help you remember the innate strength you have. And reminding yourself of your strength as a designer who lives in uncertainty will help you cope with the unknown design experience you are presently in. Telling yourself "I can make it through this," "I am strong," "I have been through design uncertainty before, and I survived," and "I can balance fear and uncertainty with problem solving and creativity" will help bring you back to the present and to the design challenge at hand. It will help you focus on solvable design actions and keep you in the present. If your mind wanders back to worrying or the feeling of uncertainty returns, refocus your mind on the present moment and engage in thoughtful internal dialogue again.

We know that as a designer, we deal with new things, experiences, and design problems and challenges. We, therefore, experience uncertainty in every stage of design. It is imperative that we become good at embracing uncertainty. If we are good at embracing uncertainty, we won't fear it. If we become comfortable with uncertainty, it's not scary. We can then embrace it and find joy in it. So how do we get good at embracing uncertainty? There are two specific tools you can use to help you embrace your uncertainty, the first is through motivation to engage and the second is through failing forward.

Engage in Uncertainty

Let's begin with your motivation to engage with uncertain situations. Uncertainty orientation is a concept that addresses your willingness to engage when presented with an uncertain situation (Rosen et al., 2014; Sorrentino et al., 2003). It identifies whether you are motivated to engage with uncertain situations to resolve them or motivated to favor situations that you are familiar with. If you are motivated to engage with uncertain situations to resolve them, the rewards of gaining new knowledge outweigh the pains associated with the feelings of uncertainty. Uncertainty orientation has been associated with differences in information seeking and processing, decision-making, and motivation to achieve (Rosen et al., 2014; Sorrentino et al., 2003). Therefore, being motivated to engage is critical for you as a designer. To help you engage in the uncertainty of design ask yourself "what's the worst-case scenario?"

If you're motivated to engage and getting out of your comfortable environment, it can be scary, but when you think about what is the worst thing that is likely to happen, usually it's not that bad. Practice experiencing the joy in the unknown. Not knowing means you are free to design with possibilities that are limitless. Being motivated to engage in uncertainty in design enables you to be in the present moment of designing, with the constant changes that take place with each decision you make and creative idea that emerges. You can embrace "not knowing" and expand your awareness to take in the dynamic complexity of design, the world, and the many ways of perceiving it.

Failing Forward

Whenever you engage in a new design, there will be times when you make mistakes, mess up, or fail. When you are designing something and it doesn't work, it is easy for you to see this as a painful failure. It is critical for the development of your designer professional identity development to look at these design failures as an important way for you to learn! (Visit Learning Segment) Failing is a way to get better at something, to grow, to get stronger. To fail forward means to purposefully and deliberately use your failure to find success (Maxwell, 2000). Failing forward requires you to do or try something new, something you want to do but might be afraid to do. Failing forward helps you to recognize the areas where you need to evolve or the things you need to change. One of the ways we can test our ideas and fail forward in design is through prototyping and/or piloting one piece of our design. Creating and testing a prototype of our design allows you to iterate or refine it repeatedly until it works. To do this, you simply take a piece of your design and give it to someone to test it out and give you feedback. Expect that they will tell you positive and negative things about your design so you can use that information to revise and improve your design. So, fail early, fail often, and fail forward.

Takeaways: Uncertainty

- Uncertainty is key to design.
- Uncertainty can serve as a threshold concept to allow you access to new pathways of knowledge.

- There are different types of uncertainty, epistemic, truth, semantic, and ontological.
- Uncertainty may influence your understanding, your behavior, and your emotions especially when it comes to creativity and decision-making.

Exercises to Cultivate Your Designer Uncertainty

1. **Create new patterns**: The purpose of this exercise is to slow your brain down. Be in the moment, not in the past, not in the future. Come up with your own "if this, then that" messages to remind yourself to shift yourself to the present moment. If a text notification, then take a breath before looking at it. If a new design proposal, then notice how your body feels as you start to read. Each intentional new pattern can shift you to a present moment approach. (Adapted from mindful.org)

2. **Journal your uncertainty**: Reflective writing is one way to help you recognize your uncertainty. When you are about to begin a new design intervention or are in any stage in the design where you feel stuck, take out your design journal and reflect on and answer one or more of these prompts:
   - How do I usually manage uncertainty?
   - How do I accept what is happening and show compassion and understanding toward myself and emotions?
   - What skills can I use in this unpredictable situation?
   - What self-care routines can I draw on to support me in this uncertain time?
   - Who can I reach out to for support and help if I need to?

3. **Reflect on past uncertainty**: Using your design journal once again, or through talking with a friend or colleague, identify one design intervention you have completed. It might not be something in your current career, it may be the design of a room in your home, a meal you made for a special group, or a party you threw to honor someone. Answer one or more of the following prompts:
   - What were the two greatest challenges I faced in this project?

- What did I do to handle those challenges before they were resolved?
- How did these challenges help me design a better project?
- How did I feel once they were resolved?
- What skills and strengths did I use in this design situation?
- What did I learn about myself?

4. **Getting through today**: Motivation to engage in your design is an important way for you to engage in uncertainty. Think about a design intervention you are currently working on. What would you like to do today in your design? It might be something small, or large, but whatever it is, your objective is to move your design forward. Before you begin your day of designing, take a moment to answer the following prompts:
   - What is my goal for today with my design?
   - What are all my options to complete this goal?
   - What obstacles might get in the way of me completing this goal today?
   - What strengths do I have as a designer?
   - How can I use these strengths to achieve my goal for today?

5. **Iterate, iterate**: When designing an innovation, the first iteration is almost never the final design. Designers go through numerous ideas, drafts, and prototypes to get to the final design. The goal of each iteration is to move the design forward, to help you as the designer embrace uncertainty knowing you are heading in the right direction. In this activity, you will create 50 short ideas, prototypes, drafts, or iterations of different ways to use a rubber band. Time yourself to come up with 50 iterations in no more than I hour. That is one idea in a little more than a minute. This will help you see how engaging in uncertainty and failing forward brings you closer to an innovative final design.

Exercises for Designers Who Teach

1. **During design, provide reflection prompts**: The purpose of this exercise is to have your design students embrace uncertainty through reflection prompts. When your

students are in the midst of a design project, provide opportunities for them to reflect on their uncertainty. Let them reflect in a way that suits their style (writing, singing, sketching, miming, etc.). Helpful prompts to get things started may include:

- How do I usually manage uncertainty?
- How do I accept what is happening and show compassion and understanding toward myself and emotions?
- What skills can I use in this unpredictable situation?
- What self-care routines can I draw on to support me in this uncertain time?
- Who can I reach out to for support and help if I needs to?

2. **Motivation board**: The purpose of this exercise is to have your design students create a visual to illustrate their goals, aspirations, and dreams as a designer. Like a vision board, this is a visual incentive that can help your students find excitement and enthusiasm to design through pictures of what they want, making it harder to ignore than words. Have your students create their Motivation Boards on a small scale, such as their motivation for a specific design intervention, to complete a course or program, or something larger like what they want to accomplish as a designer, what their designer professional identity looks like, etc. Have them take a picture and post their motivation board and place it somewhere they can see it every day they are working on a design innovation.

Energy for Your Journey

The uncertainty of design is both the frustration and joy that designers get from their activity; they have learned to live with the fact that design proposals may remain ambiguous and uncertain until quite late in the process.

(Cross, 2011, p. 12)

References

Altay, B., & Porter, N. (2021). Educating the mindful design practitioner. *Thinking Skills and Creativity, 41,* 1–19. doi: https://doi.org/10.1016/j.tsc.2021.100842

Ball, L. J., Onarheim, B., & Christensen, B. T. (2010). Design requirements, epistemic uncertainty and solution development strategies in software design. *Design Studies, 31*(6), 567–589. doi: https://doi.org/10.1016/j.destud.2010.09.003

Bar-Anan, Y., Wilson, T. D., & Gilbert, D. T. (2009). The feeling of uncertainty intensifies affective reactions. *Emotion, 9*(1), 123–127. doi: https://doi.org/10.1037/a0014607

Bosma, H. A., & Kunnen, E. S. (2001). Determinants and mechanisms in ego identity development: A review and synthesis. *Developmental Review, 21,* 39–66. doi: https://doi.org/10.1006/drev.2000.0514

Chumakovaa, M. A., & Kornilovb, S. A. (2013). Individual differences in attitudes towards uncertainty: Evidence for multiple latent profiles. *Psychology in Russia: State of the Art, 6*(4), 94–108. doi: https://doi.org/10.11621/pir.2013.0408

Cross, N. (1982). Designerly ways of knowing. *Design Studies, 3*(4), 221–227. doi: https://doi.org/10.1016/0142-694X(82)90040-0

Cross, N. (2011). *Design thinking: Understanding how designers think and work.* Berg.

Dorst, K., & Cross, N. (2001). Creativity in the design process: Co-evolution of problem-solution. *Design Studies, 22*(5), 425–437. doi: https://doi.org/10.1016/S0142-694X(01)00009-6

Dugas, M. J., Hedayati, M., Karavidas, A., Buhr, K., Francis, K., & Phillips, N. A. (2005). Intolerance of uncertainty and information processing: Evidence of biased recall and interpretations. *Cognitive Therapy and Research, 29*(1), 57–70. doi: https://doi.org/10.1007/s10608-005-1648-9

Gelmez, K., & Bagli, H. (2018). Exploring the functions of reflective writing in the design studio: A study from the point of view of students. *Art, Design and Communication in Higher Education, 17*(2), 177–197. doi: https://doi.org/10.1386/adch.17.2.177_1

Kornilova, T. V., Chumakova, M. A., & Kornilov, S. A. (2018). Tolerance and intolerance for uncertainty as predictors of decision making and risk acceptance in gaming strategies of the Iowa gambling task. *Psychology in Russia: State of the Art, 11*(3), 86–95. doi: https://doi.org/10.11621/pir.2018.0306

Lane, D. A., & Maxfield, R. R. (2005). Ontological uncertainty and innovation. *Journal of Evolutionary Economics, 15*(1), 3–50. doi: https://doi.org/10.1007/s00191-004-0227-7

Maxwell, J. C. (2000). *Failing forward: Turning mistakes into stepping stones for success.* Maxwell Motivation Inc.

Reilly, R. R., Lynn, G. S., & Aronson, Z. H. (2002). The role of personality in new product development team performance. *Journal of Engineering and Technology Management, 19*(1), 39–58. doi: https://doi.org/10.1016/S0923-4748(01)00045-5

Rosen, N. O., Ivanova, E., & Knäuper, B. (2014). Differentiating intolerance of uncertainty from three related but distinct constructs. *Anxiety, Stress, & Coping, 27*(1), 55–73. doi: https://doi.org/10.1080/10615806.2013.815743

Sorrentino, R. M., Smithson, M., Hodson, G., Roney, C. J. R., & Walker, A. M. (2003). The theory of uncertainty orientation: A mathematical reformulation. *Journal of Mathematical Psychology, 47*(2), 132–149. doi: https://doi.org/10.1016/S0022-2496(02)00032-9

Tovey, M., Bull, K., & Osmond, J. (2010). Developing a pedagogic framework for product and automotive design. In D. Durling, R. Bousbaci, L. Chen, P. Gauthier, T. Poldma, S. Roworth-Stokes, & E. Stolterman (Eds.), *Design and complexity - DRS international conference,* 1–11. https://dl.designresearchsociety.org/drs-conference-papers/drs2010/researchpapers/118

Tracey, M. W., & Hutchinson, A. (2018a). Reflection and professional identity develop-
    ment in design education. *International Journal of Technology and Design Education*,
    28, 263–285. doi: https://doi.org/10.1007/s10798-016-9380-1
Tracey, M. W., & Hutchinson, A. (2018b). Uncertainty, agency and motivation in grad-
    uate design students. *Thinking Skills and Creativity*, *29*, 196–202. doi: https://doi.
    org/10.1016/j.tsc.2018.07.004
Wang, S., & Noe, R. A. (2010). Knowledge sharing: A review and directions for future
    research. *Human Resource Management Review*, *20*(2), 115–131. doi: https://doi.
    org/10.1016/j.hrmr.2009.10.001

CREATIVITY

Hired by an international company, Makayla was tasked to design an instructional intervention for 400 workers who had no formal education or training, teaching them how to clean the largest shopping mall in the world. Her learners did not speak a common language with Makayla or each other. None of them had experience with the materials or the job tasks. She was additionally faced with a short time frame for the design and delivery of this intervention. Makayla had to imagine and design an innovative way to teach her learners, without written words or speech (Tracey & Unger, 2010, 2012). Makayla smiled and reflected, "I don't remember this chapter in my instructional design textbook."

A creative designer is one who ignores traditional ways of thinking by looking at the world in new and imaginative ways to develop original designs.

Welcome to creativity! Fold your journey map to this stop and get ready to cultivate your designer creative professional identity. Every design you

DOI: 10.4324/9781003255154-4

engage in challenges you to imagine new possibilities and produce innovative ideas to create opportunities for others to learn and grow. Like Makayla realized, there isn't a chapter for that! Ignore traditional ways of thinking or acting and create and implement original interventions.

What Is Creativity in Design?

Creativity is the ability to look at the world in new ways and turn imaginative ideas into reality. When you cultivate your creative professional identity in design, you engage in two processes: (1) thinking and (2) producing, to generate innovations. You are, therefore, engaged in creativity when something new and valuable is produced. It may be a physical product or an original idea. But, if you have ideas and don't act on them, you may be a visionary but not necessarily a creator. As a creative designer, you must put your imaginative ideas into action, producing a product resulting from those creative thoughts (Plucker & Makel, 2010).

Let's look at the first process you participate in to cultivate your creative professional identity: thinking. When you engage in creative thought, you tap into several inner resources including your insight, knowledge, curiosity, and inspiration. All your life, you have been gathering and refining these resources. Taking these thoughts and using them in extraordinary new ways is your thoughtful creativity at work.

It is not enough, however, to think creatively, you must act on those thoughts by producing something. This is the second essential process or skill to cultivate your creative professional identity in design. When you engage in the act of producing something creatively, you go beyond merely imagining to developing. Creativity includes the process of bringing something new into being. Your passion and commitment to create a novel product that is original and not predictable is creativity in practice (Fillis, 2000). Developing or producing stuff allows you to continue to develop your creative professional identity. Simply, creativity is a thought and a practice, and the more you practice, the more you develop your creative skills.

How Does Emotion Relate to Creativity?

Have you ever been told, "you must be a right brain thinker" or "the right brain is where your creativity is?" Researchers have studied creativity and mental processes in the brain, theorizing that different areas of the brain influence different types of creativity. We now know that creative thinking does not depend on any single mental process or brain region (Dietrich & Kanso, 2010). There is, however, a link between creativity and emotion so let's look at how your emotions may impact your creativity.

Have you ever thought "I am just not in the right mind to be creative right now?" Well, you were probably right as your mood, good and bad, impacts your creativity. How do we know this? Researchers conducted a series of experiments to explore the connection between mood states and creativity. Looking at both positive and negative mood and mood stimulation, they found that triggering positive moods had a positive impact on creativity through higher levels of mental flexibility. Activating negative moods improved creativity through increased perseverance (De Dreu et al., 2008). Furthermore, triggering positive emotions such as excitement supported idea creation and knowledge generation while activating negative emotions such as anger and anxiety inhibited idea creation but positively impacted persistence (Davis, 2009; Tang & Naumann, 2016). Therefore, emotion is an important source of or influence on ideation processes, including inspiration (Bonnardel & Moscardini, 2012). Negative emotions such as emotional exhaustion from sleep deprivation inhibit creativity (Han et al., 2017) while experiencing both negative and positive emotions at the same time or emotional ambivalence is an activating state and generally has a positive effect on creativity (Fong, 2006). In design, ambivalence or feeling positive and negative emotions simultaneously may be a means for fostering or promoting creative thinking (Moss & Wilson, 2014).

Furthermore, there is a strong relationship between professional identity, emotions, and creativity. Researchers discovered that designers' emotional responses to visuals, a typical source of inspiration, varied based on design expertise in that experienced designers were more likely to rate the visuals as unpleasant than less-experienced designers (Hsieh, 2014). In other words, as you develop your creative professional identity, you will find inspiration through means other than visuals. We know that emotions have a substantial influence on higher-level thinking that is important to you as a designer including creativity, judgment, decision making, and reasoning (Blanchette & Richards, 2010; Parke et al., 2015; Strickfaden et al., 2015). As you continue to develop your professional identity, you will find that as a designer you can tap into your emotions to creatively design.

Picture this. You are a part of a design team that is designing a 45-minute online training course for car dealership salespeople regarding this year's model's newest features. In the room, there is a subject matter expert, a graphic designer, a programmer, a course builder, a lead instructional designer, a script writer, and a project manager. When the instructional designer asks, "any ideas?" the blank 4 × 10 feet whiteboard comes alive with the squeaks of whiteboard markers. Empty whiteboard space is soon filled with color, sketches, key phrases, flow charts, etc. Quickly, your biggest concern becomes do we have enough whiteboard markers to go around. Design teams are influenced creatively by emotions. Researchers found that diverse teams experiencing positive emotions were more likely to be creative, while diverse teams experiencing negative emotions were less likely to be creative (Tang & Naumann, 2016). When collaborating in teams, high-arousal emotions such as excitement supported ideation while low-arousal emotions such as calmness did not, even when the feelings were positive (De Dreu et al., 2008). Emotions are a crucial feature of developing ideas, as well as in communicating those ideas to fellow design team members (Hellström & Hellström, 2003). Furthermore, positive and negative emotions are commonly found in team environments, i.e., hostility, friendly affection, and may influence individual creative performance (Yang & Hung, 2015). Design is an emotional process impacted by individual and team emotions. So, how do we keep the whiteboard markers squeaking? In his book, *Moving to Higher Ground: How Jazz Can Change Your Life*, the Pulitzer Prize-winning musician and composer Wynton Marsalis notes that whoever you are, you are creative (Marsalis & Ward, 2008). He contends that we must respect our own creativity and respect the creativity and creative space of other people. Now, where do we have more markers!

How Do I Design with Creativity?

When you begin a new design session, it may be difficult for you to tap into your creativity. There are a few things you can do, however, to increase your ability to creatively design. When you are in a positive

mood, or experiencing positive emotions, that mood tends to be associated with overall improved creativity and specifically ideation activities (Davis, 2009). Surrounding yourself with thoughts and materials
that bring you joy will help your creativity when you are engaged in
design. Think about when you feel positive in your design space. Do
you like a record spinning on your turntable, natural lighting coming
through a window, colored gel pens, your striped fuzzy socks, and/or
your favorite Starbucks beverage? When do you find yourself the most
open to creative thoughts and actions, in the mornings, afternoons, or
evenings? Are you an individual creative soul or do you prefer to create
with others? Rolling Stones guitarist Keith Richards has the astonishing
ability to write songs in his sleep. The Rolling Stones 1965 hit "(I Can't
Get No) Satisfaction" features one of the most iconic opening guitar
riffs in rock and roll history. If you have never listened to it, take a
moment now and do so. You will not be disappointed! The birth of the
riff was taped on a cassette recorder while Richards slept. Richards
awoke the next morning and listened to his recording of the intro along
with 40 minutes of snoring (Chang, 2020).

Take a moment before your design sessions to tap into what brings
you positive emotions and create that space for yourself. What if you
are not in a positive mood? Don't worry. Remember that in design
ambivalence or feeling positive and negative emotions simultaneously
may be a means for fostering or promoting creative thinking (Moss &
Wilson, 2014). The important thing then is to tap into your emotions,
identify what you are feeling and use those emotions to design with
creativity. Because design is open-ended and activates your emotional
centers, the act of designing itself is creative (Alexiou et al., 2009). This
means that the more you design the more you exercise your creativity;
therefore, design, design, design!

Remember when we started with the two processes – thinking and
producing? Let's talk about your thought process to further explain
how it can help you creatively design. "We are what we think. All that
we are arises with our thoughts. With our thoughts, we create the
world" (Buddha Quotes, n.d.). Your thoughts are powerful and when
you reflect on your personal and professional memories you are thinking about things that can inspire your design creativity. Reflecting on

your memories and experiences is a significant source of inspiration for initiating design ideas and decision-making (Ramírez, 2014; Solovyova, 2003). In the late 1980s, Phillipe Starck was a renowned designer of many products. In a new series of products designed by famous designers, Starck was asked to design a lemon squeezer (Cross, 2011). After visiting Italy to discuss the project, Starck found himself in a local pizzeria restaurant. As he waited for his food, Starck began sketching lemon squeezer ideas on the paper place mat. Sketches began a bit rough and as Starck enjoyed his antipasto plate of baby squid, his rough sketches began to shape into a squid-like lemon squeezer (Cross, 2011). Combining Starck's love of aircraft design, space rockets, science

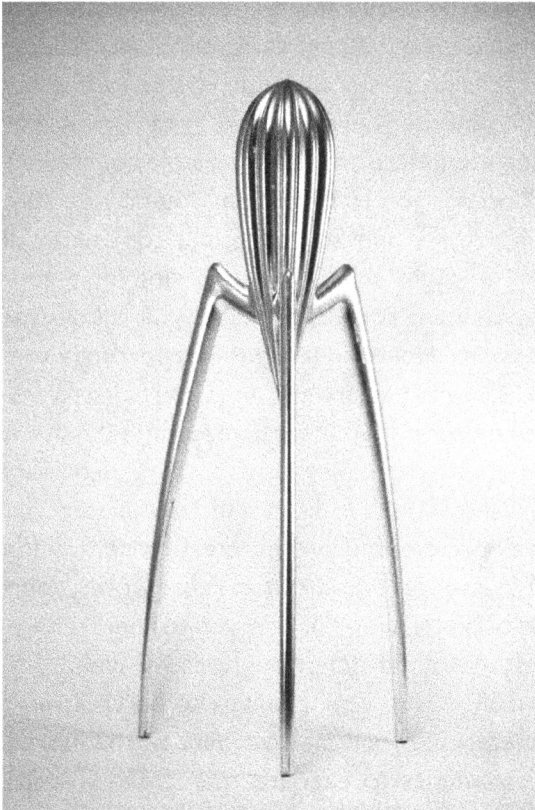

Juicy Salif lemon juicer by Philippe Starck. Designed for Alessi (1990). Originally posted to Flickr as "Juicy Salif - 78/365" by Niklas Morberg. This image is licensed under the Creative Commons Attribution-Share Alike 2.0 Generic license (https://creativecommons.org/licenses/by-sa/2.0/deed.en).

fiction, and comic strips, the aluminum retro space rocket/squid-like lemon squeezer became the *Juicy Salif.*

Knowing that focused thoughts fuel creativity, make sure to take a moment and focus your attention on what it is you want to create. Creativity requires total immersion, so you need to clear your head from outside thoughts. Give yourself the time and space you need to get completely absorbed in creativity and inspiration. Don't worry about where your thoughts take you (a plate of baby squid to a retro rocket ship to a lemon squeezer), just be open to them. This is where you allow yourself the creative space needed to design.

Your emotions and thoughts are part of who you are and your creative professional identity, specifically how you see yourself and your creative actions. When you know and are comfortable with your creative professional identity, you increase your ability to design with creativity. Your creative professional identity drives your ability to creatively design. How do you see yourself today? What is your current creative professional identity? Here are a few examples of creative professional identity behaviors for you to reflect on. You may identify as a creative designer when you are able to design in a community and when you have designer companionship. Maybe working for a good cause, feeling a purpose, or doing something meaningful is how you define your creative professional identity. Having the opportunity to be recognized and welcomed for who you are and what you bring to the table may be another way of supporting your creative identity (Endrissat et al., 2017). Your creative identity matches your creative behaviors (Lindemann et al., 2017; Werthes et al., 2018) and by the same token, creative behaviors develop and/or affirm your creative identity (Endrissat et al., 2017; Wei, 2012; Zanoni et al., 2017). In other words, your creative professional identity is one factor in how you connect with your creativity and your work. If you have a strong creative identity, you are more likely to be satisfied with opportunities to be creative. Furthermore, the more you embrace your creative identity, the more likely you will recognize opportunities to exercise your creative ability (Lindemann et al., 2017). Your creative identity is continually renewed through freedom of self-expression (Chan, 2017) and will deepen your creativity in design. When you develop your creative professional identity, you are also developing your designer creativity. Do not worry if you are early in developing your creative professional identity. An inspiring designer or a cagey veteran, you are a designer. Take your thoughts, memories, and emotions and begin to cultivate your creative professional identity.

How Do I Cultivate My Designer Creativity?

Do you remember being curious as a child? Were you someone who always asked a lot of questions? Your creativity journey began when you were born and continues to evolve through your thinking, learning, formal education, and experiences. Remember, we are all creative. So, let's keep nurturing the creativity.

If you ever tried to master something new, you know that it requires the right materials, the right environment, and a lot of practice. These tools will help you cultivate your designer creativity. Let's begin with your materials.

Select Your Materials

You are the best person to decide what materials you need for a creative design session. This may include pens, markers, crayons, colored pencils, etc., to draw and write. When deciding on something to capture and record your ideas, it might be a notebook, large chart paper, a voice recorder, a computer, or other electronic devices. You may want additional materials like music, toys, finger puppets, clay, photos, or visuals to help you relax and reflect while you are in the creative process. Collect creative materials on your designer journey. For example, you might want to collect questions you or others have asked over the years that you find interesting or compelling. If you read thought-provoking poems, short stories, essays, plays, novels, films, comic strips, and/or magazines; these are materials you might find helpful to keep on your creative journey. Reading, touching, and collecting creative materials will help inspire your designer creativity. One thing you want to make sure you have with you at all times, however, is something to record your thoughts and ideas as they emerge, so you don't forget all the ideas you generate, even when you are sleeping! A journal or something to record your thoughts whenever they emerge will help you capture your creative thoughts and ideas in real time.

Find Your Creative Environment

Only you will know what your environment should include, but there are some surroundings that support the creative process. When you design your creative environment, consider your senses. What do you want to hear, smell, or see? Do you like the sound of silence? We know that creative individuals often spend time in solitude, feel their emotions and sensations, and self-reflect while they are in the creative process. Ludwig van Beethoven was known for long, solitary walks in the woods. It is also important, however, to be open and playful. You may want to alternate between silence and turning on music or other sounds that excite or inspire you. Creativity requires innovation, and to innovate you may want to change up your normal routine. Drive to work a new way. Visit different spaces like a park, café, library, or museum. Step outside of your comfort zone, which could include changing your environment throughout your design session. You might want to start in one place, take a break and reflect and move to another location altogether. The key is to pay attention to the present moment. When you need to take a break, take a break; sleep, exercise, or enjoy any distraction that helps you to stop actively thinking about your design. Allow your unconscious mind the time needed to process what you have been creating. When you go back to your design session you might find that you have a new creative insight or breakthrough.

Practice, Practice, Practice

You have your chosen materials and your ideal environment; now it is time to practice. Developing your designer creativity requires practice, practice, and more practice. The more you practice, the greater your potential for creative output becomes. It has been shared that Thomas Edison failed 5000 times to come up with the filament of a light bulb. Creativity quantity often equals creativity quality. What this means is the longer the list of ideas you create, the higher the quality of your final intervention will be. Many times, the best idea comes at the end of your creative list! How can you become more creative? Practice by aiming for many ideas since creative geniuses often produce their best works at their times of greatest productivity. Some of your ideas will fail, but the quantity of your ideas makes it likely that other ideas will be significantly creative. Do not fear mistakes. Practice daily, experiment with ideas, learn from your mistakes, and you will cultivate your designer creativity.

Takeaways

- Creativity is the ability to look at the world in new ways and turn imaginative ideas into reality.
- When you cultivate your creative professional identity in design, you engage in two processes, 1) thinking and 2) producing, to generate innovations.
- There is a link between creativity and emotion.
- Design teams are influenced creatively by emotions.
- Your emotions and thoughts are part of who you are or your creative professional identity.
- Your creative professional identity is one factor in how you connect with your creativity and your work.
- The right materials, the right environment, and intensive practice will help you cultivate your designer creativity.

Exercises to Cultivate Your Designer Creativity

1. **Questioning**: Questions can spark your imagination and creativity. Reflect on the following questions, individually or in a group. You can also journal these questions while taking a break from a creative design session:
   a. If you were granted one wish, what would it be?
   b. If you could physically transport yourself to any place in the world at this moment, where would you go and why?
   c. If you could have any room in the world become your bedroom from now on, which room would you choose and why?
   d. If you could suddenly possess an extraordinary talent in one of the arts, what would you like it to be and what would you do with it?
   e. If you could return for one year to one age in your life, knowing what you know now, to relive that year as you

wish, which year would you go back to and what would you do differently? (Adapted from McFarlane & Saywell, 1995).

2. **Writing**: One way to tap into your emotions is through writing. Take something to write with and something to write on and find a quiet relaxing place. Set the time for 5 to 10 minutes and write everything that comes to mind. Don't hold back, don't try to make sense of what you are writing, just write down all of your thoughts. When the timer goes off, reflect on what you have written.

3. **Reflecting**: Reflect on your favorite games you played as a child. Why were they your favorite games? What did you like about them? What did you feel when you played these games? Journal your answers. Games often help stimulate creativity. Reflect on what it was in these games that may help inspire your creativity.

4. **Drawing**: Go to your local bookstore and pick up a drawing prompt book. Respond visually to a prompt provided. What could the prompt be? For example, the prompt snake scales could certainly be a detailed snakeskin, or it could be a snake slithering up to an old-fashioned scale – snake scales.

5. **Designing**: We know that one of the best ways to cultivate your creativity in design is through practice. This is also one of the best ways to improve your skills as a designer. Choose a topic, problem, or opportunity, something you would like to design an innovation for. Make sure that it is something simple, something that you can come up with a solution in a short amount of time. Commit to designing a different innovation 15 minutes every day for 30 days.

Exercises for Designers Who Teach

1. Bicycle Repair and Chopped ID are two gamified learning activities that engage designers in creatively designing with constraints. We encourage you to put your own spin on bicycle repair and chopped ID. To read how the activities work, please see Howard & Baaki (2021).

Energy for Your Journey

The best musicians know this music isn't about 'schools' at all. Like my father says, there's only one school, the school of 'Can you play?'

(Marsalis, n.d.)

Well, can you design?

References

Alexiou, K., Zamenopoulos, T., Johnson, J. H., & Gilbert, S. J. (2009). Exploring the neurological basis of design cognition using brain imaging: Some preliminary results. *Design Studies*, *30*(6), 623–647. doi: https://doi.org/10.1016/j.destud.2009.05.002

Blanchette, I., & Richards, A. (2010). The influence of affect on higher level cognition: A review of research on interpretation, judgement, decision making and reasoning. *Cognition and Emotion*, *24*(4), 561–595. doi: https://doi.org/10.1080/02699930903132496

Bonnardel, N., & Moscardini, L. (2012). Toward a situated cognition approach to design: Effect of emotional context on designers' ideas. Proceedings of the 30th European Conference on Cognitive Ergonomics - ECCE '12, 15–21. doi: https://doi.org/10.1145/2448136.2448140

Buddha Quotes. (n.d.). *Buddha Quotes*. https://www.brainyquote.com/quotes/buddha_101169

Chan, L. S. (2017). Cultivation and erosion of creative identity: A Hong Kong advertising agency as case study. *Continuum*, *31*(2), 325–335. doi: https://doi.org/10.1080/10304312.2016.1257696

Chang, R. (2020, April 27). Keith Richards wrote one of the Rolling Stones' biggest hits in his sleep. Biography. https://www.biography.com/news/keith-richards-satisfaction-rolling-stones

Cross, N. (2011). *Design thinking: Understanding how designers think and work*. Berg.

Davis, M. A. (2009). Understanding the relationship between mood and creativity: A meta-analysis. *Organizational Behavior and Human Decision Processes*, *108*(1), 25–38. doi: https://doi.org/10.1016/j.obhdp.2008.04.001

De Dreu, C. K. W., Baas, M., & Nijstad, B. A. (2008). Hedonic tone and activation level in the mood-creativity link: Toward a dual pathway to creativity model. *Journal of Personality and Social Psychology*, *94*(5), 739–756. doi: https://doi.org/10.1037/0022-3514.94.5.739

Dietrich, A., & Kanso, R. (2010). A review of EEG, ERP, and neuroimaging studies of creativity and insight. *Psychological Bulletin*, *136*(5), 822–848. doi: https://doi.org/10.1037/a0019749

Endrissat, N., Kärreman, D., & Noppeney, C. (2017). Incorporating the creative subject: Branding outside–in through identity incentives. *Human Relations*, *70*(4), 488–515. doi: https://doi.org/10.1177/0018726716661617

Fillis, I. (2000). Being creative at the marketing/entrepreneurship interface: Lessons from the art industry. *Journal of Research in Marketing and Entrepreneurship*, *2*(2), 125–137. doi: https://doi.org/10.1108/14715200080001543

Fong, C. T. (2006). The effects of emotional ambivalence on creativity. *Academy of Management Journal, 49*(5), 1016–1030. doi: https://doi.org/10.5465/AMJ.2006.22798182

Han, G. H., Harms, P. D., & Bai, Y. (2017). Nightmare bosses: The impact of abusive supervision on employees' sleep, emotions, and creativity. *Journal of Business Ethics, 145*(1), 21–31. doi: https://doi.org/10.1007/s10551-015-2859-y

Hellström, C., & Hellström, T. (2003). The present is less than the future: Mental experimentation and temporal exploration in design work. *Time and Society, 12*(2–3), 263–279. doi: https://doi.org/10.1177/0961463X030122006

Howard, C. D. & Baaki, J. (2021). Chopped ID and bicycle repair: Contrasting values in synchronous graduate instructional designs for design learning. *International Journal of Designs for Learning, 12*(2), 111–126.

Hsieh, H. Y. (2014). The influence of the designer's expertise on emotional responses. *International Conference on Human Interface and the Management of Information*, 572–582. https://www.springerprofessional.de/the-influence-of-the-designer-s-expertise-on-emotional-responses/2167920

Lindemann, D. J., Tepper, S. J., & Talley, H. L. (2017). "I don't take my tuba to work at Microsoft": Arts graduates and the portability of creative identity. *American Behavioral Scientist, 61*(12), 1555–1578. doi: https://doi.org/10.1177/0002764217734276

Marsalis, W. (n.d.). *Wynton Marsalis Quotes*. https://www.goodreads.com/author/quotes/292994.Wynton_Marsalis

Marsalis, W., & Ward, G. C. (2008). *Moving to higher ground: How jazz can change your life*. Random House.

McFarlane, E., & Saywell, J. (1995). *If... (questions for the game of life)*. Villard.

Moss, S. A., & Wilson, S. G. (2014). Ambivalent emotional states: The underlying source of all creativity? *The International Journal of Creativity & Problem Solving, 24*(2), 75–99. https://go.gale.com/ps/i.do?p=AONE&u=anon~d82b4013&id=GALE%7CA443011728&v=2.1&it=r&sid=googleScholar&asid=8ed1af15

Parke, M. R., Seo, M. G., & Sherf, E. N. (2015). Regulating and facilitating: The role of emotional intelligence in maintaining and using positive affect for creativity. *Journal of Applied Psychology, 100*(3), 917–934. doi: https://doi.org/10.1037/a0038452

Plucker, J. A., & Makel, M. C. (2010). Assessment of creativity. In J. C. Kaufman & R. J. Sternberg (Eds.), *The Cambridge handbook of creativity* (pp. 48–73). Cambridge University Press. doi: https://doi.org/10.1017/CBO9780511763205.005

Ramírez, E. R. R. (2014). Industrial design strategies for eliciting surprise. *Design Studies, 35*, 273–297. doi: https://doi.org/10.1016/j.destud.2013.12.001

Solovyova, I. (2003). Conjecture and emotion: An investigation of the relationship between design thinking and emotional content. *Expertise in Design: Design Thinking Research Symposium (Vol. 6)*. https://www.creativityandcognition.com/cc_conferences/cc03Design/papers/24SolovyovaDTRS6.pdf

Strickfaden, M., Stafiniak, L., & Terzin, T. (2015). Inspired and inspiring textile designers: Understanding creativity through influence and inspiration. *Clothing and Textiles Research Journal, 33*(3), 213–228. doi: https://doi.org/10.1177/0887302X15578263

Tang, C., & Naumann, S. E. (2016). Team diversity, mood, and team creativity: The role of team knowledge sharing in Chinese R&D teams. *Journal of Management and Organization, 22*(3), 420–434. doi: https://doi.org/10.1017/jmo.2015.43.

Tracey, M. W., & Unger, K. L. (2010). Cross cultural instruction: An instructional design case. *International Journal of Designs for Learning, 1*(1). doi: https://doi.org/10.14434/ijdl.v1i1.845

Tracey, M. W., & Unger, K. L. (2012). A design-based research case study documenting a constructivist ID process and instructional solution for a cross-cultural workforce. *Instructional Science, 40*(3), 461–476. https://www.jstor.org/stable/43574696

Wei, J. (2012). Dealing with reality: Market demands, artistic integrity, and identity work in reality television production. *Poetics: Journal of Empirical Research on Culture, the Media and the Arts, 40*(5), 444–466. doi: https://doi.org/10.1016/j.poetic.2012.07.002

Werthes, D., Mauer, R., & Brettel, M. (2018). Cultural and creative entrepreneurs: Understanding the role of entrepreneurial identity. *International Journal of Entrepreneurial Behavior & Research, 24*(1), 290–314. doi: https://doi.org/10.1108/IJEBR-07-2016-0215

Yang, J. S., & Hung, H. V. (2015). Emotions as constraining and facilitating factors for creativity: Companionate love and anger. *Creativity and Innovation Management, 24*(2), 217–230. doi: https://doi.org/10.1111/caim.12089

Zanoni, P., Thoelen, A., & Ybema, S. (2017). Unveiling the subject behind diversity: Exploring the micro-politics of representation in ethnic minority creatives' identity work. *Organization, 24*(3), 330–354. doi: https://doi.org/10.1177/1350508417690396

ETHICS

Makayla develops her professional designer identity in different ways. One way is by actively listening to podcasts. Sitting down with a cold glass of iced tea and a piece of raspberry cheesecake, Makayla popped in her AirPods and listened to Hanna Harris (Stella, 2021) discuss how design is helping Helsinki, Finland transform its future. Ms. Harris explained that the aim is to use design to develop Helsinki as the most functional city in the world. What is making a difference in Helsinki is that design is not just about designed objects, but how people relate to objects and use those designed objects. Between bites of cheesecake, in her design journal, Makayla jotted down trust, transparency, openness, how people relate to things and services, and foresight thinking. After the podcast, Makayla thought about what Ms. Harris called citizen engagement. The idea that citizens are cocreators and that designers come to know and understand citizens. Makayla took a sip of iced tea and thought, "How can I design a world that brings sustainability in activities every day?"

DOI: 10.4324/9781003255154-5

Design constitutes being human.

Take a deep breath. Another. One more. Smile. You have put some memorable miles behind you, and there are still so many glorious miles ahead as you cultivate your designer professional identity. Maybe, you have read the segments in order. Or, you have come up with your own segment order based on your current designer situation. Either way, bravo to you! This is how we designed the segments. With that said, the ethics segment and the diversity, equity, and inclusion segment complement each other. In the ethics segment, we reference a localized context of use and the 3 Is, which in the diversity, equity, and inclusion segment we dive deep into the frameworks of both. If you have participated in the diversity, equity, and inclusion segment, then the ethics segment will take a localized context of use and the 3 Is to another level. If you have yet to pore over the diversity, equity, and inclusion segment, you may want to first discover the ethics segment and then move to the diversity, equity, and inclusion segment. Your journey. Your choice. Now, let's help Makayla reveal how we can design a world that brings sustainability in activities every day.

How Does "It's Not What It Is. It's What It Means" Relate to Design?

Klaus Krippendorff (2006) writes about a semantic turn in design. Design is making sense of things, and design is a turn toward considerations of meaning. Krippendorff further explains that product semantics is an inquiry into how people attribute meaning to stuff and interact with stuff. He contends that we act according to the meaning of whatever we face. Therefore, a design artifact means what its context permits. We act on how we sense a design artifact. We act on what an artifact means to us, and we act on what we want to accomplish from the artifact. In sum, Krippendorff (2006) states, "Design constitutes being human" (p. 74).

Arturo Escobar (2017) writes about the emerging tendencies in the design world. The traditional meanings of design practice were linked to objects, technological change, individuals and markets, and experienced experts carrying out the design of objects. Escobar shares that a new conception of design, focused on the audience, is situated, interactive, collaborative, participatory, and focused on the production of the human experience and life itself. In a localized context of use approach, we have described this conception of design as designing for the moment.

Makayla reflected on what Escobar (2017) asks, "How, then, can one design a world that brings forth flourishing (sustainability) in everyday activities" (p. 123). Escobar answers that it is all about the notion of care (self, others, world) where care is structured into the design of tools and equipment through "presencing" (p. 123). For your designer professional identity, presencing combines a localized context of use with Tonkinwise's (2013) conception of designing little stuff a lot, all over (visit the diversity, equity, and inclusion segment). Escobar suggests presencing is going beyond designing with a goal of satisfying an audience's needs. Presencing is designing to articulate the concerns of a collectivity in novel ways where new embodied routines become collective, "...eventually transforming social consciousness and institutional structures" (p. 123). So, what does presencing have to do with designing with ethics?

What Is Good and What Is Bad? How Does My Designer Professional Identity Ethics Decide?

Merriam-Webster (n.d.) defines ethics as dealing with what is good and bad and with moral duty and obligation. First and foremost, designing with ethics means designers must make ethical choices. Manzini (2006) professes that designers thrive in the openness of a field of possibilities. Manzini warns that socio-technical conventions may dictate where there is no choice which means design does not happen. To Escobar (2017), socio-technical conventions are institutional structures. Manzini (2006) digs deeper as socio-technical conventions are "complex mixtures of implicit knowledge, customs and mores" (p. 13). Manzini further explains that socio-technical conventions are a slow co-evolution of technology and society. The challenge comes when, "increasing speed of change generates discontinuity and break-down in conventional wisdom because what must be done, how and by whom, can no longer be taken for granted" (p. 13). When this happens, a demand for design emerges.

Back to designers must make ethical choices. In design, we act. Manzini points out that our choices that lead to action are more than our intentions. When we make design decisions, we must consider the results and implications of our decisions. Designing with ethics for sustainability means designing for wellbeing.

What Is Product-Based Wellbeing?

Is product-based well-being (Manzini, 2006), democratic access to all products, a strong and good idea? Certainly. Is it sustainable? Now, that is a bit complicated. Manzini (2006) explains it like this. Twenty percent of the population consumes 80% of available resources. If this were to change and the other 80% succeeded in product-based wellbeing, we would face an ecological disaster. However, if this does not happen, we face a social disaster. As Manzini notes, a highly interconnected and globalized society cannot endure only 20% access to a promised well-being while 80% of people have no chance to participate in the wellbeing. Is the answer halfway between the two? Maybe, or maybe not. Would we face simultaneously an ecological and social crisis? Manzini concludes that there would be increasing high impact consumers at the same time as potential resource consumers being excluded. Looking through a lens influenced by Krippendorff, Escobar, and Manzini, how do we design for sustainable well-being where all live well while consuming less? How does this impact your designer professional identity?

The Jardin Nomade

In a quiet residential part of Paris, an eyesore plot of land was transformed into a locally run garden, meeting, and event space (Davis, n.d.). Making sure there is always something happening in and around the garden, residents, families, and schools care and cultivate the vegetable garden. A professional gardener supervises the garden, distributes plots of land, gives gardening advice, programs activities, and undertakes environmental research. City hall assists by loaning the site and providing water and electricity infrastructure, waste management service, and equipment like soil, growing boxes, and fencing.

Regarding social wellbeing, Jardin Nomade has inspired inter-generational interaction, involvement with schools and associations and has created a healthier environment. Young graffiti artists painted a mural on the Jardin Nomade back wall bringing in interested young people who interact with elderly citizens and families finding roles and exchanging expertise.

For environmental wellbeing, the Jardin Nomade supports a Paris policy for sustainable development by encouraging local consultation and participation and greening Paris. Within the policy, sites must respect the environment, develop biodiversity, and encourage the young, especially, to develop environmental and civic responsibility.

Sustainable Housing and Living Project De Kersentuin

A group of people were inspired to live in a socially and ecologically sustainable neighborhood that did not exist (Zaalberg, n.d.). The city of Utrecht, Netherlands was willing to help. The sustainable neighborhood has environmentally friendly houses for diverse groups of people, with good interaction between neighbors, lots of social activities, and where everything is organized by the neighborhood. Houses use sustainable materials, solar power, and environmentally friendly ventilation systems. Neighbors take initiative for all activities and services like car sharing, using handcarts, and maintaining bicycles.

In benefitting the society, there are few cars in the neighborhood which results in a more child-friendly place. The neighborhood is diverse and there is a lot to do which brings and keeps people together. The neighbors are innovative, and they feel more like a whole community.

Environmentally, the neighbors designed a car-sharing project. Neighbors maintain green spaces. Neighbors share facilities like environmentally friendly washing machines, and neighbors have designed systems to provide an economic use of solar cells for energy and rainwater for domestic use.

How did Project De Kersentuin and Jardin Nomade bring sustainability in everyday activities? It was not at macro-level interventions, but rather at micro-level interventions. Manzini (2006) calls it local radical discontinuities, or "…systemic changes with regard to a given context, in the sense that they challenge traditional ways of doing and introduce a new set of different (and intrinsically more sustainable) ones" (p. 13). For you, triggering and supporting local radical discontinuities is a choice, not an obligation.

How Do I Cultivate My Ethical Designer Professional Identity?

Although there are numerous ways to develop your ethical designer professional identity, one thing you can do today is trigger and support local radical discontinuities. Triggering and supporting local radical discontinuities rely on us taking a localized context of use approach through introspection, interaction, and intention (the 3 Is). Manzini (2006) shares three guidelines: (a) promote wellbeing, (b) enable people to live as they like and in a sustainable way, and (c) enhance social innovation and steer toward more sustainable ways of living. Before getting into each guideline, let's review the 3 Is and a localized context of use. Explore the diversity, equity, and inclusion segment for a detailed journey through the 3 Is and a localized context of use.

Although one side of a localized context of use approach is all about reflection and empathy for the audience and for you as the designer. The other side of a localized context of use is all about action. If we are designers of change, we must reflect on our own context and those of the given circumstances and then act. The 3 Is (introspection, interaction, and intention) (Thomas et al., 2002) drive a localized context of use where you decide the specific moment of use and design for the moment (Herman et al., 2022). Designing to promote wellbeing, enabling people to live as they like, and enhancing social innovation are not merely theoretical aspirations, but rather tangible deliverables.

Promote Wellbeing

Manzini (2006) explains that designers promote well-being by involving those whom the designer designs for. The audience of focus becomes a co-producer of results as the audience of focus knows what they want to achieve. Why involve the audience of focus? Manzini notes that the audience of focus brings necessary intellectual and practical resources and knows best the specific problem or opportunity that requires an intervention. When promoting wellbeing, provide an environment where the audience of focus fulfills their potential using their skills, knowledge, and abilities to get results (Manzini, 2006).

Introspection is about educating ourselves and connecting with our audience on a deep and personal level. In the Hanna Harris Podcast regarding Helsinki, Finland, Makayla found it interesting that Ms. Harris talked about citizen engagement. Makayla saw how citizen engagement impacts Helsinki's design goal of becoming the most functional city in the world. When we interact with our audience of focus (interaction), we collaborate to determine specific moments of use. Considering a specific moment of use, we then can reflect on how our audience will use our design and numerous ways our audience may act. When we determine the specific moment of use, we design for the moment and promote wellbeing.

Enable People to Live as They Like and in a Sustainable Way

In designing with ethics for sustainability, Manzini (2006) is adamant that designers must move from designing to solve problems to designing to enable people to live as they like. Here, interaction is paramount as the audience of focus has a role and the designer has a role. Interaction between designer and the audience of focus leading to action (intention) results in creative communities (Manzini, 2006) where people cooperatively invent, enhance, and manage innovative interventions for new ways of living. Reflect on what is happening with the sustainable housing and living project De Kersentuin. People came together to design a socially and ecologically sustainable neighborhood that, prior, did not exist. The De Kersentuin neighbors did not approach the neighborhood as a problem. They determined that their specific moment of use was a neighborhood where houses use sustainable materials, neighbors take initiative for all activities, share cars and washing machines, and design systems to use solar cells for energy and rainwater for domestic use. What is most evident here is the neighbors acted.

Enhance Social Innovation and Steer Toward More Sustainable Ways of Living

For Manzini (2006), creative communities and social innovation go hand in hand. Here is where within a localized context of use, the 3 Is come together to make an impact, and the designer emerges as the expert. The designer interacts with the audience of focus in a peer-to-peer collaboration. The designer is an expert with specific design knowledge and specific design skills (Manzini, 2006). Design knowledge involves finding a balance between the macro-situation (how things have changed and are changing) and the micro-situation (a localized context of use approach). With design skills, a designer promotes and enhances introspection, interaction, and intention in new contexts, facing the new challenges. For Jardin Nomade, a professional gardener (an expert designer in their own right) supervises the garden, distributes plots of land, gives gardening advise, programs activities, and undertakes environmental research.

Takeaways: Ethics

- Traditional meanings of design practice were linked to objects, technological change, individuals and markets, and experienced experts carrying out the design of objects.
- A new conception of design, focused on the audience, is situated, interactive, collaborative, participatory, and focused on the production of the human experience and life itself.
- Designing with ethics means designers must make ethical choices.
- Local radical discontinuities are systemic changes regarding a given context. Local radical discontinuities challenge traditional ways of doing and introduce a new set of different ways of doing.
- Trigger and support local radical discontinuities by promoting wellbeing.
- Trigger and support local radical discontinuities by enabling people to live as they like and in a sustainable way.
- Trigger and support local radical discontinuities by enhancing social innovation and steering toward more sustainable ways of like.

Exercises to Trigger and Support Local Radical Discontinuities

1. **Create your finder**: Take a piece of paper and cut out a rectangle to simulate a camera viewfinder. With your finder, take a walk in your neighborhood, downtown, your city park, or your favorite nature trail. Crop your world! Look through your

viewer and discover all the things that you never bothered to notice. (Adapted from Kleon, 2019)

2. **Triggering and supporting local radical discontinuities #1**: More of a design concept than a set design, an Earthship (Grout, n.d.) is made from natural and recycled materials, like used tires and aluminum cans. An Earthship is powered by renewable energy, such as wind, water, and solar power, catches rainwater for its water supply, and treats and contains its own sewage in planter beds. An Earthship can be adapted for any climate in the world. People build their own homes and decide to live lightly on the earth. The purpose of the Earthship is to inform people that they can, simply, reduce their impact on the environment. Imagine you are involved with the Earthship. Reflect on the following prompts:

   • Describe how you would help promote well-being working with those who live in the Earthship.
   • How would you move from designing the Earthship just to solve an environmental problem to designing the Earthship to allow people to live as they like?
   • How would you enhance the creative community?

3. **Triggering and supporting local radical discontinuities #2**: A group of elderly people did not feel comfortable living alone and even less comfortable living in an elderly home. So, they came up with an initiative for an elderly living society (Rutten, n.d.). Aquarius is a social community of older people (between 55 and 65 years old in order to have a mix of older and younger neighbors) who want to grow old together. Seniors have their own private home and garden, as well as a communal space and large communal garden. Neighbors help each other out as much as possible. Aquarius is a community where elderly people can spend their days in a very social active environment. It is a throwback to a time when neighbors were good friends and helped each other out when they are sick or just need some assistance. Some residents lived on their own and felt lonely, with little or no social connections to society. Others felt insecure in their own houses and wanted to feel safe. Still others need regular healthcare atten-

tion but did not want to go to an elderly home. Imagine you are involved with Aquarius. Answer the following prompts:

- How would a localized context approach impact Aquarius' sustainability?
- How do the 3 Is ensure the right choices are made for Aquarius' continued success?

4. **What is good and what is bad?** Technology has such an impact on how we design. Take artificial intelligence (AI) for example, the opportunities are endless. But, what about deepfake videos? If you are not familiar with deepfake videos, take a minute to look it up. Reflect on the ethical choices you may have to make regarding deepfake videos? What other technology tools do you see promoting wellbeing, enabling people to live as they like, and enhancing social innovation? Reflect on the tools' impact for designing with ethics for sustainability.

Exercises for Designers Who Teach

1. **Field Trip!** Have your designers create a viewfinder by cutting a rectangle out of a piece of paper (2 inches/5 cm x 1 inch/2.5 cm). Now that the designers have their own camera viewfinder load them up and take them on field trip. It could be anywhere. Downtown. A local manufacturing plant. A low-income housing project. A farmers' market. Have each student use their viewfinder to crop the world, seeing for the sake of seeing. Encourage designers to discover things that they have never bothered to notice. Remind them that their cropped world is not what the cropped world is, but rather, what the cropped world means. Also, remind them that design constitutes being human. (Adapted from Kleon, 2019)

   Have the designers reflect:
   - What does the cropped world mean to me?
   - What may the cropped world mean to those who are part of the cropped world?
   - For those who are part of the cropped world, what may they want to accomplish?
   - For my cropped world, how can I design with ethics to bring forth sustainability in everyday activities?

> ### Energy for Your Journey
>
> *Act so that the effects of your actions are compatible with the permanence of genuine human life.*
>
> (Jonas, 1984, p. 11)

References

Davis, L. (n.d.). *Jardin nomade*. EMUDE. http://www.sustainable-everyday-project.net/emude/?p=194

Escobar, A. (2017). *Designs for the pluriverse: Radical interdependence, autonomy, and the making of worlds*. Duke University Press.

Grout, I. (n.d.). *Earthship fife*. EMUDE. http://www.sustainable-everyday-project.net/emude/?p=55

Herman, K., Baaki, J., & Tracey, M. W. (2022). "Faced with given circumstances": A localized context of use approach. In B. Hokanson, M. Exter, M. Schmidt, & A. Tawfik (Eds.), *Toward inclusive learning design: Social justice, equity, and community*. Springer.

Jonas, H. (1984). *The imperative of responsibility*. The University of Chicago Press.

Kleon, A. (2019). *Keep going: 10 ways to stay creative in good times and bad*. Workman Publishing.

Krippendorff, K. (2006). *The sematic turn: A new foundation for design*. CRC Press.

Manzini, E. (2006). Design, ethics and sustainability. Guidelines for a transition phase. University of Art and Design Helsinki, 1–8. http://designblog.uniandes.edu.co/blogs/desis/files/2009/06/060828-design-ethics-sustainability.pdf

Merriam-Webster. (n.d.). *Merriam-Webster.com dictionary*. https://www.merriam-webster.com/

Rutten, D. (n.d.). *Aquarius, social elderly community of age 55+*. EMUDE. http://www.sustainable-everyday-project.net/emude/?p=168

Stella, O. (Host). (2021, July 29). *Hanna Harris on how design can help develop a functional city*. In *Design Core Detroit Podcast*. https://designcore.org/detroit-city-of-design/podcast/?mc_cid=f1e4914cb1&mc_eid=4b6bf7bfb5

Thomas, M., Mitchell, M., & Joseph, R. (2002). The third dimension of ADDIE: A cultural embrace. *TechTrends*, 46(2), 40–45. doi: https://doi.org/10.1007/BF02772075

Tonkinwise, C. (2013). It's just going to be a lot of hard work - Four problematic and five potential ways of accomplishing radical sustainability innovation. DRAFT. Retrieved from https://uts.academia.edu/camerontonkinwise

Zaalberg, J. (n.d.). *Sustainable housing and living project De Kersentuin*. EMUDE. http://www.sustainable-everyday-project.net/emude/?p=211

DIVERSITY, EQUITY, AND INCLUSION

Twice a month, Makayla meets her good friend Clare for coffee. Clare works for a community college and sits on the retention and completion committee as well as a committee that is tasked to streamline tutoring services. On this coffee date, Clare was overwhelmed. Clare shared that when analyzing who uses the free one-to-one tutoring a two-fold gap surfaced. Overall, male students account for 40% of the student body, but only 27% of the tutoring population. Furthermore, African-American males make up 32% of the student population and 60% are not utilizing tutoring services. Clare added that the tutoring website is difficult to navigate, students cannot choose their tutors, and less than 15% of tutors are African-American males. Clare pleaded to Makayla, "Where do I start? How do I get my arms around something so big with its societal, educational, and political implications? How do we better market the tutoring services to our African American male students?" Makayla was sensitive to Clare's situation and thought out loud; it is not about what the tutoring services are, but rather, what the tutoring services do for African American male students.

DOI: 10.4324/9781003255154-6

Design for moments of use, a lot, all over.

A Radical Kind of Empathy?

Take a seat and reflect on your journey map concerning designing interventions around situations of inequity, a lack of diversity, and/ or non-inclusion. Can you relate to Clare's situation? Right away are overwhelmed and uncertain two words that come to mind? As Clare noted, "Where do I start?" We are going to focus on how you can get your arms around, and design for situations of inequity, a lack of diversity, and/or non-inclusion. While you participate in the segment, we encourage you to reflect on your diversity, equity, and inclusion views. In fact, if you want to start with the reflection, Exercise #6 under Exercises to Develop your Localized Context of Use will guide you.

Wilkerson (2020), in her best-selling book *Caste: The Origins of Our Discontents*, suggests that we all have a duty to develop a radical kind of empathy for those who endure inequity or non-inclusion. A radical kind of empathy includes educating ourselves and listening with a humbled heart to understand another's experience from their perspective, not as we would imagine another would feel. According to Wilkerson (2020), a radical kind of empathy involves growing a 'kindred connection" (a deep knowing that opens our spirit) to the pain of another as they perceive the pain (p. 386). Finally, a radical kind of empathy means we *act* when we see others treated unfairly.

Stop, just for a moment. Reflecting on your designer professional identity journey, you may ask out loud, "is this really a *radical* kind of empathy?" Great question! In your adventures thus far, you see how empathy threads through so much of what makes you a designer. Your designer professional identity is evolving to where opening yourself in a responsive way to others' feelings and experiences is *the way* you design. Your empathic design approach includes a strong, fibrous thread that weaves your design interventions. What becomes essential to designing interventions that address situations of inequity, lack of diversity, and non-inclusion is effectively acting on an issue that seems just too big. It takes a lot of work. Let's explore.

Trying to Turn an Aircraft Carrier

Clare was right. Her design situation has cultural, societal, socioeconomic, political, and educational implications. At first glance, her situation is like trying to turn an aircraft carrier: it takes a lot of force, it is slow, and it takes a long time to turn such a huge ship with such momentum. Tonkinwise (2013) reframes a societal issue as a problem that is, "…ingrained because it manifests at a small-scale, in the semi-conscious everyday activities of billions of households and workplaces around the world" (p. 1). Changing situations of inequity, a lack of diversity, and/or non-inclusion involves changes to everything we do every day. Tonkinwise (2013) calls it radical sustainable design which means, "designing little things a lot, all over" (p. 14).

What Are the Two Sides to a Localized Context of Use?

Designing a lot of little things, here there and everywhere means you must get your arms around a specific context involving inequity, a lack of diversity, and/or non-inclusion. The word context is rooted in *contextere* which means to weave together. How you attend to and organize your perception of a situation is an important part of context. A localized context of use emphasizes specific moments of use where context is scaled back to what is needed in a moment (Baaki & Tracey, 2019; Herman et al., 2022; MacPhail, 2014; Meloncon, 2017). In other words, when you shrink the scale of context (MacPhail, 2014; Meloncon, 2017), you identify the critical forces at work that can affect how you approach the design.

Take the United States' opioid overdose crisis. The crisis is a complex network of socioeconomic, political, social, cultural, and medical issues. Bivens (2019) presented how the Chicago Recovery Alliance (CRA) and PwrdBy attempted to decrease deaths by opioid overdoses. The successes of a community-based approach (CRA) and technology-based approach (PwrdBy) were based on designers understanding the opioid users', who often feel excluded, context of use. As Bivens (2019, p. 18) put it:

> Knowledge about opioids, legal repercussions, and opioid illicitness might contextually factor into any user's decision-making process when asking for help in instances of opioid OD (overdoses), meaning the contexts and realities in which these users make decisions are integral elements to consider when designing health information for these situations.

A deeper dive into a localized context of use leads us to two sides of a localized context of use. A localized context of use emphasizes a personal side of context (Meloncon, 2017) where a designer reflects on their context and the context of those of the circumstance (Baaki & Tracey, 2019). On the flip side, a localized context of use approach is more than having empathy for the audience. A localized context of use results in action. Let's look at both sides.

Localized Context of Use Emphasizes a Personal Side of Context

Our audience of focus acts in context and we, as designers, act in context. Your personal side of context and your audience's personal side of context are dynamic, about interpretation, filling spaces, and meaning making to move forward. The following figure represents how these four elements weave together for a personal side of context.

Marcie has been a practicing dental hygienist for 10 years and is completing her Master of Science in dental hygiene. Marcie aspires to teach dental hygienists at a community college. As part of her master's

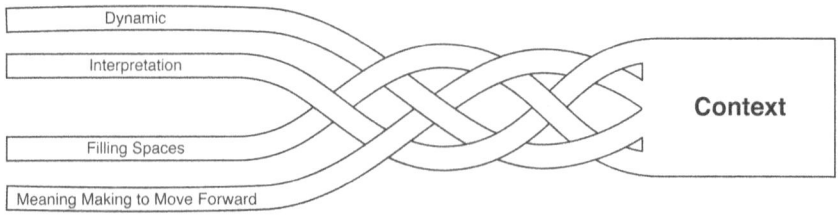

The personal side of context.

program, Marcie took a non-instructional intervention design course. Inspired by the course and reflecting on her evolving designer professional identity, Marcie wanted to reach out to her community and design an in-school elementary program for third to fifth graders regarding the importance of brushing their teeth. She chose an elementary school where at-risk children do not have equitable access to affordable dental care. Marcie reflected on the personal side of context.

A Personal Side of Context Is Dynamic

Visiting Broad Street Elementary School, in Mr. Wilder's health and physical education class, Marcie met Jacqueline, a precocious fourth grader who is the middle child of three. Jacqueline's mom, a single parent, works nights cleaning an office building. Nothing in Jacqueline's life is stationary. While mom works four 10-hour shifts per week, Jacqueline, her older brother, and younger sister find themselves staying with relatives and friends during the nights that mom works. Each week, Jacqueline may stay with an aunt one night, grandma for two nights, and mom's best friend another night. Each night means a different bed to sleep in, different room to do homework, and a different routine to get ready for bed.

As Marcie gets to know Jacqueline, Marcie realizes that nothing about designing is stationary. As a designer developing her professional identity, Marcie experiences epistemic uncertainty (Ball et al., 2010). Marcie is aware of what she knows: children need to develop good dental hygiene. Marcie is also aware of what she does not know about her design space: why isn't Jacqueline developing good teeth brushing habits. This motivates Marcie to learn about Jacqueline's challenges in brushing her teeth regularly. Marcie is gaining insight into the nature and boundaries (Dorst & Cross, 2001) of the dental hygiene problem at Broad Street Elementary School.

A Personal Side of Context Is about Interpretation

MacPhail (2014) contends that context is synonymous with interpretation. Jacqueline is a smart fourth grader. In the personal health lesson of her health and physical education class, Mr. Wilder discussed the importance of staying healthy by eating right, washing up every night, and brushing your teeth twice a day. Jacqueline thinks about her week, and how brushing her teeth twice a day is difficult. Her bedtime and wakeup time varies at each place she stays, and often she forgets to pack her toothbrush in her overnight bag.

Even though Marcie is a dental hygienist, she draws on her experiences as a young dental hygienist working for a family dental office. Marcie would often begin an appointment with a young patient with a true and false game. True or false, you brush your teeth once a day. True or false, you brush your teeth twice a day. Unbeknownst to her young patients, Marcie knew the answers by just peeking inside the youngsters' mouths. Using her early experiences as a dental hygienist to understand her design challenge is an example of designer precedents (Baaki & Tracey, 2015; Tracey & Boling, 2014). Marcie interprets her values and beliefs structures (dental hygiene is critical to good health), prior experiences (children struggle brushing regularly), and knowledge and skills (experienced hygienist working on a master's degree) as she makes her design decisions.

Personal Side of Context Is about Filling Spaces

Jacqueline uses her fourth grader life experiences as a lens to view unfolding events and make sense of everyday events. Jacqueline actively participates in an exchange of context (MacPhail, 2014) with Mr. Wilder, her mom and siblings, her teachers, family, and friends. Exchange of contextual information has pragmatic and operational value as it changes Jacqueline's context so she can create her own meaning (MacPhail, 2014). What does this mean? Jacqueline's grandma, better than anyone else, makes certain that Jacqueline brushes her teeth prior to going to bed. Mr. Wilder stresses that Jacqueline needs to brush her teeth in the morning and at night. Jacqueline is bright enough to understand what brushing her teeth twice a day means (what brushing-twice-a-day information is). What Jacqueline wants to do is figure out how the brushing-twice-a-day information fills the space in her setting, staying away from home four days a week.

Marcie is empathic to Jacqueline's situation. We know this because Marcie visited Mr. Wilder's class at the Broad Street Elementary School and befriended Jacqueline. Marcie is filling in the spaces about how good dental hygiene is affected by Jacqueline's context. By being sensitive to

Jacqueline's situation, she is closer to Jacqueline's and the other students' daily life which will increase the likelihood that the importance of brushing teeth program will meet the Broad Street fourth graders' moments of use when they brush their teeth.

Personal Context Is about Meaning Making and Moving Forward

MacPhail (2014) might explain what Jacqueline is trying to do (be an excellent fourth grader and a healthy fourth grader) as a creative synthesis of personal knowledge and impersonal data. Mr. Wilder has provided information (impersonal data) that brushing your teeth twice a day results in healthy teeth and a healthy student. Jacqueline knows that it is difficult to maintain a consistent teeth brushing schedule and that it is a chore to make sure she has a toothbrush in her overnight bag (personal knowledge). Making meaning of impersonal data and personal knowledge helps Jacqueline to move forward.

Marcie reflects on her 10-year experience as a hygienist and the children that have sat in her dental chair. Marcie is grateful to meet Jacqueline and understand her situation. Marcie's combined personal, educational, and professional experiences create meaning for her brushing teeth project. Now, Marcie affectively forecasts, predicting Jacqueline's and the Broad Street students' affect (emotional state) about being a fifth grader and beyond (Tracey & Hutchinson, 2019). She reflects on how the Broad Street fourth graders will feel after they complete the program. Marcie's meaning-making helps her move her design to action.

How Do I Design with Diversity, Equity, and Inclusion?

Remembering that a localized context of use emphasizes specific moments of use where context is scaled back to what is needed in a moment (Baaki & Tracey, 2019; Herman et al., 2022; MacPhail, 2014; Meloncon, 2017), the way to shrink the scale of context (MacPhail, 2014; Meloncon, 2017), and act is through the 3 Is of a localized context of use.

The 3 Is and a Localized Context of Use

A localized context of use approach does not simply mean reflection and empathy for the audience and for yourself as the designer. As designers of change, we must reflect on our own context and those of the given circumstances and then we must act. Thomas et al. (2002) introduced the 3 Is – introspection, interaction, and intention. The 3 Is drive a localized context of use such that you determine the specific moment of use and design for the moment (Herman et al., 2022). Designing to change inequity, a lack of diversity, and/or non-inclusion is not theoretical, but rather tangible.

Designing with Introspection

Marcie has closely examined the context surrounding Jacqueline's and the Broad Street fourth graders' specific moment when they are able to brush their teeth. Marcie is designing with introspection. Marcie reflects on how she understands Jacqueline's situation. Marcie identifies the critical forces at work that affect her understanding of why Jacqueline and her friends do not always brush their teeth each day. By befriending Jacqueline and visiting Broad Street Elementary School, Marcie educated herself, connected, and communicated with her audience on a deep and personal level. True, Marcie considers other stakeholders – Mr. Wilder and other teachers, Broad Street Elementary principal, parents, and her dental colleagues. But, to move the needle forward for at-risk children who do not have equitable access to affordable dental care, Marcie designs for Jacqueline and her friends, not the teachers, not the principal, and not the parents.

Designing with Interaction

Marcie interacted with Jacqueline and the Broad Street fourth graders. Marcie, first, considered why the children do not brush their teeth twice a day. In addition to Jacqueline presenting her position, other children explained that they have never been to the dentist and never had a toothbrush of their own. Trevor shared that his parents never taught him to brush his teeth. Miguel sheepishly confessed that he has a toothbrush but forgets to brush his teeth as no one reminds him. Collaborating with the fourth graders to understand what is happening at the moment when the students should be brushing their teeth is helpful for Marcie as she designs an intervention. As Marcie designed her program, she began to reflect on how Jacqueline and her friends will use the program and the ways the students may act. In other words, when designing with interaction, it is not enough to consider what is happening at the moment of use. We need to consider what *will* happen at the moment of use once the design is developed and implemented. When Jacqueline took into account what will happen, her program began to take shape and went from an idea to something tangible. She was now designing with intention.

Designing with Intention

One side of a localized context of use is reflection and the other side of a localized context of use approach to design is action. Designing with intention means our intent is to act. If we are going to push the needle toward a more diverse, equitable, and inclusive society, we design for the moment of use at our workplace, in our neighborhood, at our place of worship, at Broad Street Elementary School, and a lot of other places. Marcie determined what was happening at the moment of use when the Broad Street fourth graders should be brushing their teeth and designed for the moment. Marcie's *Brushing Broadly for Me* program kicked off the new school year with much success. Jacqueline's and her classmates designed their own brushing schedules focusing on how many times they brush their teeth not on when they brush their teeth. Each student received two toothbrushes; one for home and one in a travel bag that each student decorated. Toothpaste and dental floss also were included in the bag. Marcie worked with teachers and the principal to introduce an incentive program where students earn points if they follow their brushing schedules. When the class meets a goal, the class gets to participate in special events like a guest speaker from a county dairy farm who shares how milk makes teeth strong and a visit to a county apple orchard where Jacqueline and her friends learn how an apple a day keeps the dentist away. Finally, Marcie arranged for a nearby dentist office to participate in a state grant to offer low-cost dental care for all the Broad Street Elementary families.

Are the 3 Is a Design Model with Three Distinct Steps?

Emphatically, no! In our experience working with and instructing designers, when a design team is in a design collaboration moment, the team bounces, often at a quick pace, introspection, interaction, and intention all around the room. Imagine three lasers where introspection is red, interaction is blue, and intention is yellow in a closed room. As each laser, continuously and rapidly, bounces off walls, ceiling and floor, the lasers cross one another, then bounce around individually, then cross again, then singularly bounce, then cross some more, and so on. When introspection, interaction, and intention cross, it may be a design break-through moment for the team, or it may be a moment where the team realizes they need to go back to one of the 3 Is and take a closer look. In design, we may refer to this as abductive thinking. Designers shift and transfer thought between an activity's required function and purpose and an intervention's appropriate forms to satisfy the purpose (Cross, 2011). Treating the 3 Is as a three-step model where you work through introspection, then interaction, and finally intention mars how the 3 Is drive a localized context of use approach.

How Do I Cultivate My Designer Radical Kind of Empathy for DEI?

In presenting her radical kind of empathy, Wilkerson (2020) asks, "... what is it that human beings do when faced with a given circumstance" (p. 387)? Let's reframe the question. What is it that designers do when faced with a given circumstance of inequity, a lack of diversity, and non-inclusion? We allow introspection, interaction, and intention to come together to break the back of inequity, a lack of diversity, and non-inclusion (Herman et al., 2022). Inspired by a radical kind of empa-thy, we design moments of use, a lot, all over (Tonkinwise, 2013). We put in the hard work to educate ourselves and listen humbly to under-stand another's experience from their perspective (Wilkerson, 2020). We search for a connection from a place of deep knowing that opens our spirit to the pain and suffering of another as they perceive the pain and suffering (Wilkerson, 2020). In sum, we act when we see another person treated unfairly (Wilkerson, 2020).

Takeaways: Diversity, Equity, and Inclusion

- A radical kind of empathy means we *act* when we see others treated unfairly.

- Changing situations of inequity, a lack of diversity, and/or non-inclusion involves changes to everything we do every day.
- A localized context of use approach does not simply mean reflection and empathy for the audience and for yourself as the designer.
- Introspection, intention, and interaction (the 3 Is) drive a localized context of use such that you determine the specific moment of use and design for the moment.

Exercises to Cultivate Your Localized Context of Use

1. **First listen, then reflect!** As you scour your news feeds, your favorite websites, or just look around your world, when people are faced with given circumstances of inequity, non-inclusion, and a lack of diversity educate yourself and listen humbly to understand their experience from their perspective. Reflect on your understanding in whatever way that helps you to connect and communicate in a deep and personal way. Draw, journal, video, or quietly reflect.

2. **The 3 Is – Introspection**: Tina realized that her family lived in a book desert – a geographical area where reading materials are difficult to obtain. A map of her city showed a literacy redline between those neighborhoods with access to books and those without. Tina's neighborhood is diverse with affordable housing built only blocks from million-dollar homes. Tina's family chose the neighborhood because of its diversity, but being that her family is white, from out of state, and live in a newer home, Tina realizes that her family is part of gentrification in her city. Her family plans to start a Little Free Library in front of her home. Reflect on the following prompts:
   - What is the context surrounding the specific moment of the intervention – starting a Little Free Library?
   - Identify the critical forces that can affect the understanding and use of a Little Free Library.
   - In order to move forward, how would you educate yourself and connect and communicate with the people in Tina's neighborhood on a deep and personal level?

3. **The 3 Is – Interaction**: Margaret works at a Title I school which is part of a U.S. federal program that supports low-income students. Her school does not offer any extracurricular activities. Margaret remembers her elementary school years where she was part of an after-school art club. In fact, today, Margaret continues to take art classes and paints. She has witnessed that her students show an interest in art. Knowing that in order to move the needle toward a more diverse and inclusive school, Margaret must keep her design idea small and within her circle of influence. Margaret plans to create a weekly after-school art club that meets once a week for eight weeks. Students will learn about four different cultures and will create art reflecting the cultures. Each student will choose an art piece to be displayed at the local library. Answer the following prompts:
   - How can Margaret interact with the students to determine what the students will get out of creating artwork that reflects different cultures?
   - Consider what the students are facing right now with no extracurricular activities. What are the students' current moments of use?
   - How may the students use the art club? How may they act as they participate?

4. **The 3 Is – Intention**: As a chemistry and robotics teacher at Plainsville High School, you contend that diverse teams are more likely to reach scientific and technological innovations because those with diverse perspectives envision different solutions. Plainsville High School is 82% African American, Asian American, and Latinx American. You intend to create a STEM program focused on robotics as part of the school's Academies of Plainsville. The STEM program will provide female students and students of color, who face equity issues when it comes to STEM, with an opportunity to learn how engineering, physics, and technology interrelate in the world of robotics. You also see an opportunity for students to experience firsthand how diverse

teams can do great STEM things. Take a moment to answer the following prompts:
- What is the specific moment of use for the students who participate in the robotics program?
- How would you design the robotics program for the moment of use?
- Consider that your design is tangible instead of just theoretical.

5. **The 3 Is – Introspection, interaction, and intention**: At a physical therapy center, a patient intake form (PIF) collects information for both the billing department and the therapists to establish a medical record. A PIF also fulfills a legal obligation to inform patients of their rights and responsibilities. Oftentimes, PIFs are designed without considering a patient's moment of use – completing the form prior to an appointment. Not considering a patient's perspective may make the patient feel they are in the wrong place to get the care they need. A patient who has a sprained ankle experiences completing a PIF much differently than a patient who struggles with a neurological disease that makes writing difficult, or a patient with excruciating back pain who cannot tolerate sitting to complete lengthy forms. A general outpatient physical therapy center cares for patients with diverse disabilities. Font size, language, means of delivery (written vs. digital), information required, and when the form is completed affect a patient's experience.
   - Grab some scrap paper and design a PIF.
   - Take a localized context of use approach and apply the 3Is to your design. Let the lasers bounce around!

6. **Then and now**: In a notebook, on a walk, in a poem, or however you see fit, reflect on your past and current views on diversity, equity, and inclusion. How have your views evolved? How do your evolving views impact your design work?

Exercises for Designers Who Teach

1. **Move the Needle!** Design for moments of use, a lot, all over: With your designers, reflect on how they can commit to diver-

sity, equity, and inclusive excellence? What interventions can they design to close gaps in non-inclusion, inequity, and a lack of diversity? Here are some possible guides for the designers:

- Designers may work alone or may team up; no teams greater than three
- Let designers choose a project
- Keep it small; keep it local; keep it within your circle of influence
- How do you design constructive action? How do you move the needle to a more diverse, equitable, and inclusive society in your neighborhood, organization, and/or city, not sure we want to go bigger than that?
- Have students work through the 3 Is
- Have designers share drafts and final designs with other designers
- Now we can help drive hope! Find the hope! Embrace the hope! Engage in the hope!

Energy for Your Journey

The secret is being like children and like water: joyful, transparent, creative, and in movement.

(Escobar, 2017, p. 166)

References

Baaki, J., & Tracey, M. W. (2015). Repertoire of precedents: Designers kindling fatwood during reflection is action. In B. Hokanson, G. Clinton, & M. W. Tracey (Ed.), *The design of learning experience: Creating the future of educational technology* (pp. 155–166). Springer.

Baaki, J., & Tracey, M. W. (2019). Weaving a localized context of use: What it means for instructional design. *Journal of Applied Instructional Design, 8*(1), 2–13. https://253f0a53-bb62-46af-b495-b4548f4d5d90.filesusr.com/ugd/c9b0ce_d055972f6f-b942098860aac6071cc11e.pdf

Ball, L. J., Onarheim, B., & Christensen, B. T. (2010). Design requirements, epistemic uncertainty and solution development strategies in software design. *Design Studies, 31*(6), 567–589. doi: https://doi.org/10.1016/j.destud.2010.09.003

Bivens, K. M. (2019). Reducing harm by designing discourse and digital tools for opioid users' contexts: The Chicago Recovery Alliance's community-based context of use and Pwrdby's technology-based context of use. *Communication Design Quarterly, 7*(2), 17–27. doi: https://doi.org/10.1145/3358931.3358935

Cross, N. (2011). *Design thinking: Understanding how designers think and work.* Berg.

Dorst, K., & Cross, N. (2001). Creativity in the design process: Co-evolution of problem-solution. *Design Studies, 22*(5), 425–437. doi: https://doi.org/10.1016/S0142-694X(01)00009-6

Escobar, A. (2017). *Designs for the pluriverse: Radical interdependence, autonomy, and the making of worlds.* Duke University Press.

Herman, K., Baaki, J., & Tracey, M. W. (2022). "Faced with given circumstances": A localized context of use approach. In B. Hokanson, M. Exter, M. Schmidt, & A. Tawfik (Eds.), *Toward inclusive learning design: Social justice, equity, and community.* Springer.

MacPhail, T. (2014). *The viral network: A pathography of the H1N1 influenza pandemic.* Cornell University Press.

Meloncon, L. K. (2017). Patient experience design: Expanding usability methodologies for healthcare. *Communication Design Quarterly, 5*(2), 19–28. doi: https://doi.org/10.1145/3131201.3131203

Thomas, M., Mitchell, M., & Joseph, R. (2002). The third dimension of ADDIE: A cultural embrace. *TechTrends, 46*(2), 40–45. doi: https://doi.org/10.1007/BF02772075

Tonkinwise, C. (2013). It's just going to be a lot of hard work - Four problematic and five potential ways of accomplishing radical sustainability innovation. DRAFT. https://uts.academia.edu/camerontonkinwise

Tracey, M. W., & Boling, E. (2014). Preparing instructional designers: Traditional and emerging perspectives. In J. M. Spector, M. D. Merrill, J. Elen, & M. J. Bishop (Eds.), *Handbook of research on educational communications and technology* (4th ed., pp. 653–660). Springer. doi: https://doi.org/10.1007/978-1-4614-3185-5_52

Tracey, M. W., & Hutchinson, A. (2019). Empathic design: Imagining the cognitive and emotional learner experience. *Educational Technology Research and Development, 67*(5), 1259–1272. doi: https://doi.org/10.1007/s11423-019-09683-2

Wilkerson, I. (2020). *Caste: The origins of our discontents.* Random House.

REFLECTION

Makayla is a diverse music lover. One of her favorite artists is Lorde. Makayla was excited to relax, sit back, and listen to Lorde and David Byrne of Talking Heads fame participating in Rollingstone's Musician on Musician segment (Rollingstone.com, 2021). For 40 pleasurable minutes, Makayla listened as Lorde and David Byrne swapped stories on fighting stage fright, remaining true to their inspiration, and uncovering the mysteries of song-writing. Makayla was struck on how naturally both Lorde and David spoke about what they do as musicians. She also found it interesting that both musicians often confessed that they never thought about the questions that one another asked. Both just want to make music, and that is what they do, make music. After the episode, Makayla took a minute to reflect on how much she learns from her designer colleagues when they share their design stories. She thought, "It is one thing to reflect on my own design experiences, it is something different to listen to other designers' experiences. There is so much to learn from both."

DOI: 10.4324/9781003255154-7

As practitioners of a profession, we do a lot of things professionally that just feel so obvious, natural, or self-evident that we don't hesitate at all or think about what we are doing. We just do them.

Reflection. You have been reflecting quite a bit as you have put Segments behind you. One thing you know for certain is reflection is a big part of cultivating your designer professional identity. This segment will be no different. You will be reflecting on how you reflect. As Makayla realized, it is one thing to reflect on your design experiences, and it is something different to listen to other designers' experiences. Both are important to your designer professional identity. Enjoy reflecting on, well, reflecting.

What Is Reflection and What Is Its Role in Design?

Precisely defining reflection is difficult. Rooted in the work of John Dewey, reflection is an active and ongoing process of contemplating your beliefs, experiences, and forms of knowledge (Tracey et al., 2014). Reflection emphasizes personal and internal knowledge construction through recursive considerations and interpretations of your experiences and beliefs (Tracey et al., 2014). True, we most often think of reflection in terms of problem solving. When we expand reflection to include a way to define and redefine our beliefs, values, and perspectives, reflection becomes a crucial tool for the formation of our designer professional identity (Tracey et al., 2014).

Why Do Designers Find It So Hard to Reflect?

Design schools focus their curriculum on the premise that design is something that you must learn (Dorst, 2003). By experiencing designing and reflecting upon your experiences, you learn what design is and how to do it (Dorst, 2003). Design schools ask you to reflect explicitly and communicate your thoughts to your instructors and design colleagues. Dorst (2003) argues that this is a difficult task. Reflecting requires that you are fully aware of your design experiences, able to communicate them explicitly, select the most relevant experiences, find patterns in the experiences, and then reflect on the experiences considering the "how" and "why." This does not include coming up with ideas for a new approach on your next design project (Dorst, 2003).

Think about it (excuse us, reflect on it) for a moment. Your design projects are very different, and therefore, it becomes difficult to take experiences from one design project to the next design project. Hutchinson and Tracey (2015) found that even for designers who have significant experience, discussing how design ideas emerge is difficult. In developing a professional identity, Wackerhausen (2009) suggests, "As practitioners of a profession, we do a lot of things professionally that just *feel* so obvious, natural, or self-evident that we don't hesitate at all or think about what we are doing. We just do them" (p. 461). Wackerhausen further points out that developing professional identity can hamper professional collaboration. Through habit, we find ways to talk, explain, perceive, value, do, and assume, which often conflicts with our neighboring professions. Wait, there is hope. Although articulating internal processes in a design space can be challenging, research with teacher education students shows that reflection-on-action (we will discuss later) may have a positive effect on belief changes that support students in assimilating new experiences and constructing a professional knowledge framework (Tracey et al., 2014).

How Do Explicit and Implicit Reflection Affect My Designer Professional Identity?

Since the early 1990s, reflection has been emphasized such that a reflective practitioner is an ideal practitioner (Wackerhausen, 2009). Although reflection has historical roots in the work of John Dewey, Donald Schön's book *The Reflective Practitioner* (1983) has strongly impacted designers' worlds by making expressions like reflection *in* practice and reflection *on* practice familiar to designers (Wackerhausen, 2009). However, not everyone agrees that professional or expert practitioners should be reflective practitioners (Wackerhausen, 2009). The argument goes that only novices and beginners need to think about what they are designing. Expert designers will do what needs to be done, and they will not think about what they are doing. So, do we glorify reflection or dismiss reflection?

To answer, we need to look at how a designer reflects, and the kind of reflection that happens (Wackerhausen, 2009). Before we walk deeper into the woods, it is important to agree that designers at least will reflect sometimes. So, reflection is not a question of to reflect or not. Wackerhausen (2009) argues that in our everyday design life what becomes topics of reflection are the constraints, obstacles, and hindrances to our everyday practice. In other words, what we reflect on is not our everyday design road, but what is blocking the road. Designers will reflect sometimes as we confirm, not challenge, our road of everyday design practice. But what kind of reflection has the potential to challenge and transform our everyday design road?

An Anatomy of Reflection

Before we explore implicit and explicit reflection, we need to establish the basic anatomy of reflection. Wackerhausen (2009) contends that the different varieties of reflection are constituted by four elements. First, when we reflect, we always reflect *on* something (a theme, a problem, idea, etc.). Second, when we reflect on something, we reflect *with* something (certain concepts, beliefs, data, etc.). Third, we reflect *from* something (a certain interest, a perspective) when we reflect on and with something. Finally, when we reflect on, with, and from something, we also reflect *in* something (a context, a surrounding).

Let us return to one of Makayla's favorite artists, Lorde, participating in *Rollingstone's* Musician on Musician segment. Lorde reflects on what she loves best, making music. Reflecting on her music, Lorde reflects with the influence of David Byrne's music on what Lorde does when writing a song. Lorde reflects from her interest that David Byrne's music is timeless when Lorde reflects on the music she makes with Byrne's influence on Lorde. Finally, when Lorde reflects on her music, with the influence of Byrne's music from the interest that Byrne's music is timeless, Lorde reflects in a context where she can be totally open and vulnerable about her musical journey.

Explicit Reflection

Your designer professional identity includes an understanding of your-self in a design situation and what is expected of you in the design space (Hutchinson & Tracey, 2015). To fully see yourself as a designer, you must know what design is, what designers do, and who you are as a designer (Hutchinson & Tracey, 2015). Who you are as a designer is influenced by your personal traits, habits, talents, and limitations. Engaging in explicit and implicit reflection helps you develop your designer professional identity.

Recall your last design project. What did you reflect on while you were designing? As you designed potential solutions, did the design problem become clearer or, maybe, even change? How did reflecting on the co-evolution of the problem and intervention change your final design deliver-able? What about constraints? As you reflected on constraints like budget and project deadlines, how did constraints affect what you designed? Once you completed the design deliverable, what did you reflect on that will help you with your next design? Your reflection was explicit.

Explicit reflection is engaging in reflective conversations with the design problem and tentative solutions in order to better understand the relationship between the two (Tracey & Hutchinson, 2018). Studying reflection by language teachers, Gerlach (2021) concludes that teachers first need a philosophy of teaching that is shaped by who the teacher is. Also necessary are teaching principles that guide a teacher through the language teaching process. When a teacher acts, justified by teaching theories, their practice then allows for reflection while they practice. Reflection becomes recursive. Gerlach (2021) explains, "Reflection, which is embedded in situational contexts, is created anew every time a professional acts and is therefore highly context-specific" (p. 41).

Tracey and Hutchinson (2018) investigated the use of reflective writ-ing in an introductory design course to help students better understand their design belief, experiences, and self-awareness. A study implication was that the complex problems designers face and their designer pro-fessional identity are embedded in the design students' design thinking, design decisions, and design outcomes. In other words, there is a close connection between reflecting during design (explicit reflection) and reflection on designer identity (implicit reflection).

Implicit Reflection

Gordon Ramsey is an internationally renowned and multi-Michelin starred chef. He has restaurants across the globe from the United Kingdom to France to Singapore to the United States. His television shows include Kitchen Nightmares, Hell's Kitchen, Hotel Hell, and MasterChef US. Gordon is a truly remarkable designer of delicacies. If you have watched one of Ramsey's television shows, you will notice that Gordon often invites guest chefs where he engages with the guest chefs humbly asking them how they got started designing food and who and what inspired their cooking styles. These discussions represent master chefs implicitly reflecting. Designers cannot get enough of listening to design stories (Dorst, 2003). Share a design story. Listen to a design story.

Wackerhausen (2009) contends that a practitioner must become a stranger to themselves. Being a stranger to themselves means obtaining knowledge of and becoming familiar with concepts, theories, ideas, and knowledge outside of a designer's profession. When a professional practitioner is a stranger to themselves, Wackerhausen (2009) states that the practitioner can, "…describe the familiar in unfamiliar terms and from unfamiliar perspectives and consequently, to become a stranger to herself and attain a desirable degree of alienation" (p. 467). In other words, if you sat down with Gordon Ramsey, even though you are not a chef, what would you gain from cooking design that you could use in your design field?

Gerlach (2021) proposes that teachers may reach a level of implicit reflection through narrative prompts. Gerlach suggests that in the reflective narratives what is most important is how teachers write about their practice and actions. The challenge for the teaching profession is to understand what is happening through a dialogic process. Gerlach (2021) concludes that implicit reflection is collaborative involving discussion and dialogue with a colleague or critical professional friend. Focusing on instructional designers, Tracey et al. (2014) provide support to Gerlach noting that reflection is a crucial tool for the formation of professional identity. Cultivating designer professional identity materializes from narratives and reinterpretations of relevant experiences that support conceptions of a professional identity. Listen to a design story. Share a design story.

How Do I Reflect to Keep Cultivating
My Professional Identity?

Simply put, to keep cultivating your designer professional identity, you need to reflect. Hutchinson and Tracey (2015) concluded that emerging instructional designers need support in developing their identity and maintaining their identity's presence in reflective activities. The support can occur through multiple opportunities to reflect in professional knowledge, experiences, and action as well as feedback on how to maintain presence in reflective activities. You need to keep working on your professional identity.

There are many reflection techniques and methods. If reflecting individually, try a reflective diary, portfolio, or reflective writing (Gerlach, 2021). If you are reflecting with someone else, you may engage in peer coaching, learning conversations, or mentoring (Gerlach, 2021). Visualizing may be effective via videography or conceptual maps while venturing into experimental reflection may lead to simulations (critical incidents) or creating tasks for other professionals and overseeing the execution of the tasks (Gerlach, 2021). What may be most important to your implicit and explicit reflection development is when and how you reflect-in-action, reflect-on-action, and reflect-for-action. Let's look at each one separately.

Reflect-in-action

When you are designing, you may produce a sketch, model, conceptual map, spreadsheet, or some other type of external representation or draft. You stand back and take stock in your external representation. Your external representation speaks to you. Through recursive reflection on the external representation, you realize changes that are needed for your intervention and you better understand the design problem. Schön (1983) introduced such reflection as reflection-in-action. Reflection-in-action refers to an ongoing internal dialogue that you have while you are designing where you interpret and re-interpret contextual factors in light of your experiences, beliefs, and knowledge to make design decisions and move forward to a design deliverable.

Reflect-on-action

Once you have produced your design deliverable, you may have a formal or informal evaluation process to determine your deliverable's value. Formal or informal, you are reflecting on the final design deliverable. Schön (1983) explained reflection-on-action as the construction and revision of narratives and explanations surrounding prior practices, experiences, and beliefs. Revising narratives and explanations is personal and results in reinterpretations as the designer gains new knowledge. In sum, you are reflecting on what has happened already.

Reflect-for-action

In this segment, we have stressed that reflection is essential to your designer professional identity development. When we draw on past design experiences when considering what could happen for future design actions, we are reflecting-for-action (McAlpine & Weston, 2000). You reflect-for-action more than you think. When you design, you are creating something new. You are developing something that had not existed prior to receiving a design brief. Embracing your design stories and others' design stories becomes relevant when you design for what could happen (Tracey et al., 2014).

Reflection means accountability. Within your design space, you reflect to examine the design context with discipline, to invent and re-invent processes, and to take responsibility for your design decisions (Tracey et al., 2014). Reflection (before, during, and after the design context) is the connection between the design problem and the ultimate design intervention. Consistently reflecting on your design experiences, beliefs, values, and knowledge is the starting gate for your design judgments, decisions, and actions (Tracey et al., 2014). Now, reflect on that!

Takeaways: Reflection

- Reflection emphasizes personal and internal knowledge construction through recursive considerations and interpretations of your experiences and beliefs.
- The different varieties of reflection are constituted by four elements: (a) we always reflect *on* something, (b) when we reflect on something, we reflect *with* something, (c) we reflect *from* something when we reflect on and with something, and (d) when we reflect on, with, and from something, we also reflect *in* something.

- Who you are as a designer is influenced by your personal traits, habits, talents, and limitations.
- Cultivating designer professional identity materializes from narratives and reinterpretations of relevant experiences that support conceptions of a professional identity.
- Reflection-in-action is an ongoing internal dialogue that you have while you are designing where you interpret and reinterpret contextual factors in light of your experiences, beliefs, and knowledge.
- Reflection-on-action is the construction and revision of narratives and explanations surrounding prior practices, experiences, and beliefs.
- Reflection-for-action is drawing on past design experiences when considering what could happen for future design actions.
- Reflection means design accountability.

Exercises to Cultivate Designer Reflection

1. **Reflect on a recent design project**: Open a notebook or a sketch book and reflect on a recent project. What were your constraints? How did you design to your constraints? What was the problem/opportunity? What was your solution/intervention? How did you get to the solution/intervention? Share your story with another designer. What perspective does your colleague share?
2. **Reflect on one part of your designer identity**: Describe a time when you felt totally uncertain. Remember how that felt and the greatest challenges you faced because of the uncertainty. Reflect on what you did to handle the uncertainty? Knowing that uncertainty is part of your designer professional identity, how do you feel? [Adapted from Tracey et al. (2014)]
3. **A reflection dinner party**: You are hosting a night of food and drink that will begin at 6:00 P.M. and go well into the early hours of the next day. Your three guests are designers (maybe musicians, engineers, painters, chefs, architects, etc.) who are still designing today. You have asked each guest to bring something that they have designed to share with the rest. You also

contribute something you have designed. Who are your three dinner guests? What design are you going to contribute to the dinner party? What is the story behind your design?

Exercises for Designers Who Teach

1. Research indicates that reflective writing assignments are a way to support students as they explore design concepts, experiences, and beliefs, which provide a foundation for students' emerging designer professional identities (Tracey et al., 2014). When assigning design projects, provide students with opportunities to develop reflective skills. Allow them to reflect explicitly as they design. Provide students with reflection prompts during and after the design is complete. Allow them to reflect implicitly. If the design project is a team project, have design teams share their stories with one another. If students designed alone, create reflection teams and have team members share and listen to the design stories.

Energy for Your Journey

You can never hear enough design stories. It is always nice to learn from other designers' mistakes, so that you might not have to make so many yourself.

(Dorst, 2003, p. 81)

References

Dorst, K. (2003). *Understanding design: 150 reflections on being a designer.* Bis Publishers.

Gerlach, D. (2021). Making knowledge work: Fostering implicit reflection in a digital era of language teacher education. *Language Education and Multilingualism - The Langscape Journal, 3,* 29–51. doi: https://doi.org/10.18452/22340

Hutchinson, A., & Tracey, M. W. (2015). Design ideas, reflection, and professional identity: How graduate students explore the idea generation process. *Instructional Science, 43*(5), 527–544. doi: https://doi.org/10.1007/s11251-015-9354-9

McAlpine, L., & Weston, C. (2000). Reflection: Issues related to improving professors' teaching and students' learning. *Instructional Science, 28*(5), 363–385. doi: https://doi.org/10.1023/A:1026583208230

Rollingstone.com (host). (2021). Lorde and David Byrne [Video episode]. In *Musicians on Musicians.*

Schön, D. A. (1983). *The reflective practitioner: How professionals think in action.* Basic Books, Inc.

Tracey, M. W., & Hutchinson, A. (2018). Reflection and professional identity development in design education. *International Journal of Technology and Design Education, 28,* 263–285. doi: https://doi.org/10.1007/s10798-016-9380-1

Tracey, M. W., Hutchinson, A., & Grzebyk, T. Q. (2014). Instructional designers as reflective practitioners: Developing professional identity through reflection. *Educational Technology Research and Development, 62,* 315–334. doi: https://doi.org/10.1007/s11423-014-9334-9

Wackerhausen, S. (2009). Collaboration, professional identity and reflection across boundaries. *Journal of Interprofessional Care, 23*(5), 455–473. doi: https://doi.org/10.1080/13561820902921720

LEARNING

Makayla was stuck. As a designer on the team creating a leadership team building event, she could not see the design. Every idea the team came up with seemed old and tired, done a million times before. The company's leaders were hard working and divisive, determined, and independent. They had no desire to work together for fear of losing their power and their position. The company executives, however, realized if their leaders did not become a team, the company would lose. This was an important client. How could Makayla and the design team bring them together? Makayla left her office to clear her head and as she walked, she came upon a school playground. She observed the children playing kickball, negotiating the rules, choosing teams, and winning and losing. She watched them agree, disagree, and work out the challenges of playing together. She remembered her own high school softball team and what worked and what didn't work as they made a run for the state title. Suddenly, it came to her. She knew exactly what her team needed to design to make the company's leaders a team.

Designers learn from education and experience, from practice and observation, from success and failure.

Welcome to learning. Fold your journey map to this stop and get ready to embrace the joy and excitement you will experience as a continual learner. Design is ever evolving and as a designer, it is your responsibility to constantly cultivate yourself and your abilities. Learning from success, failure, and from others directly impacts your ongoing designer professional identity development. Like Makayla, you may draw from your past experiences as a shortstop. You may stop and observe the dynamics of a playground kickball game. You will always observe others and reflect on your successes and failures as you continue to learn how to design. For you as a designer, learning is central to your designer growth. So, settle in because it is time to explore how ongoing learning cultivates your designer professional identity. Let's get started!

What Is Learning?

As a designer, you have put miles behind you on your learning journey. Your inborn designer characteristics and your formal design education have guided you to this point, but this is only the beginning of cultivating your professional identity. Learning is identified as enduring change but how do we learn? Designers learn from education and experience, from practice and observation, and from success and failure. Through ongoing learning, you continue to gain knowledge and improve your design skills. Learning is active and social, enhanced by collaboration and interaction, while deep learning is challenging, meaningful, purposeful, and engaging. To be an accomplished designer, you must take ownership and participate in all forms of learning throughout your entire design career.

How Is Design Learning?

Kenneth Grange began his design career in large part by accident. After completing four years at an art school on a scholarship, he was introduced to an alumnus who secured him a position in a leading architectural firm although he had never heard of architecture. Grange has become one of the most accomplished innovative designers in large part because of his ongoing desire to learn. He credits his ability to self-teach, his inquisitive nature, and his general interest in mechanics and structures for his success as a designer. His popular design of the Frister & Rossman sewing machine was completely re-envisioned because he engaged with the machine. By actually learning how to use the machine, he identified its strengths and frequent problems. Grange learned through his experience with the sewing machine, then re-designed an innovative style with unique features (Cross, 2011). Kenneth Grange learns through design.

Take a moment and think about how *you* design. What is the first thing *you* do? While you gather knowledge about the design problem, the audience you are designing for, and the best approach toward a design solution, you are engaging in learning. Learning is change, and by attempting to change something through design, you are engaging in designing as a means to learn.

As a designer, you may begin a new project by looking at what is needed in an effort to discover and clarify what the problem really is. You gather as much information as you can, look at the problem from different perspectives and you might try experimenting with some initial solutions. You may propose an idea and then sketch it, look at it with a critical eye, and have others look at it as well. You learn from that initial feedback and reflection and change your preliminary ideas in an effort to improve your design and then you look at it again. Design is a process of going through many of these *learning cycles* (propose-experiment-learn) until you have created a solution. What you are doing is learning your way toward a design (Dorst, 2003; Lawson & Dorst, 2009). So, design by its very nature is learning.

Why Do Designers Need to Constantly Learn?

Steve Jobs dropped out of Reed College in his first year and became one of the most influential designers of the 21st century (Isaacson, 2011). How did he learn how to design? As a child, living in Los Altos, CA, Jobs helped his father build a fence. When he questioned why they were taking painstaking effort to make sure the fence was the same on the back, where no one saw it, as on the front, visible to all, his father remarked that he and his son would know how it looked on the back. Jobs used this learning experience when designing the Apple products as an adult, learning how to make them as beautiful on the inside as on the outside. He used this previous life experience as the basis for new learning.

Learning through Previous Life Experience

Think back to the games you played, the friends you had, and the food you liked as a child. Did you travel with others, read pleasure books, play team sports? Did you have a series of jobs, favorite classes in school, or experiences at summer camp? All of these previous life experiences influence how you currently learn. Experiences build on one another and whenever you start something new, it is important for you to draw on your previous life experience. So, your current learning is informed in part by your past learning. To support new learning, it will help you to begin by reflecting on your life experiences. You may choose to document these memories, in written or oral form. The important thing to remember is your life experiences are the foundation for new learning.

In the mid-1970s, Steve Jobs studied the principles of Zen Buddhism which emphasize simplicity. Jobs reflected on the most fundamental form of Zen art, the hand-drawn circle, which inspired his mouse design years later. Jobs learned through experiential learning. Let's dive a bit deeper.

Learning through Concrete, Reflective, Abstract, and Active Experience

Experiential learning (Kolb & Fry, 1975) can support your goal as a life-long learning designer. The four stages in the experiential learning cycle provide you with the chance to loop through a continuous learning experience. We begin with concrete, which is the actual experience you participate in. For Jobs, it was actually experiencing the teachings and practice of Zen Buddhism. You then engage in reflection and abstraction where you observe and conceptualize learnings from that experience. Jobs reflected on the hand-drawn circle several years later when designing the computer mouse, which is the last stage in experiential learning, activation, or experimentation. So, you begin with the actual experience, reflect, and abstract learning from it and use that reflection and abstraction for action or experimentation (Lawson & Dorst, 2009).

While visiting a local department store in Palo Alto, CA, Steve Jobs studied household appliances, especially the Cuisinart. He was so enamored by this design that he made every member of his design team purchase one to study the lines, curves, and bevels of the machine. The designers then began to experiment with clean lines, curves, and bevels as they attempted to design the personal computer. Jobs and his designers learned through design practice.

Learning through Practice

As a designer, you will actually learn and develop best through ongoing design practice (Lawson & Dorst, 2009). Situated learning (Lave & Wenger, 1991), the learning through practice that is highly social learning, takes place in the very context in which the learning is to be applied. In other words, it is the actual space *where* you learn that is just as important as *what* you learn. Since we know that design practice is most often done in groups or teams, the *where* the learning takes place is in the social and interactive context of designing with others. Learning through practice becomes part of a social relationship and cultivates your professional identity (Lawson & Dorst, 2009). When working in a design team, the entire team learns and develops individual and collective expertise. Learning from actual design practice and through design projects are the most important ways to learn through practice.

Having all of the skills required to be successful in your design field can seem elusive and if you believe that you are not yet prepared, you are not alone. Industrial design employers expressed their dismay as design graduates rarely have the skills required to be successful (Yang et al., 2005). Rather than specific training in technologies, something their formal education provides, employers stressed the need for less tangible abilities like design thinking, communication, and an ongoing interest in design (Yang et al., 2005). They believe that an overemphasis in design education on learning specific technologies does not support learning responsibility (Alhajri, 2016), and technologies become obsolete quickly (de Bont & Liu, 2017; Yang et al., 2005). Other employers, however, were found to be dismayed when newly hired design graduates lacked specific technological skills (de Bont & Liu, 2017; Yang et al., 2005).

How is it possible to learn everything you need to know in your design education program to successfully design? It's not! It is impossible to walk out of your formal education with all of the skills you will need to be a designer. Remember the multiple ways Steve Jobs learned and be ready and excited for a career that includes endless learning. Like Jobs, learning through life experience, experiential learning, and by design practice contributes to the cultivation of your designer professional identity.

How Do I Learn from Failure?

Acclaimed fashion designer Marc Jacobs came out of school as the winner of numerous fashion awards and was the youngest designer to ever win the Council of Fashion Designers of America (CFDA) Perry Ellis Award for new Fashion Talent. While working for another designer, he created a collection that received such terrible reviews that he was immediately fired and as far as the fashion industry was concerned, he was finished as a designer. Today, he is one of the world's most celebrated designers.

It can be difficult and painful to fail, but the truth is failing is an opportunity for personal and professional growth. Truth or folklore, the story goes that Thomas Edison failed 5000 times to come up with a filament for his light bulb. An assistant asked Edison when he was going to quit. Edison responded that he did not know what the assistant was talking about. He had discovered 5000 things that do not work. Just like experiencing success, experiencing failure is an important part of life since without failure, we would be less capable of feeling great accomplishment. It is through failure that we learn some of our greatest personal and professional lessons.

During the Apollo 13 space flight, Gene Krantz, the director of the mission control team on the ground made the statement that "failure is not an option" (Slegers et al., 2012). Although this statement was made to describe the fate of the Apollo 13 astronauts, there is an overall expectation in our culture that demands immediate success.

We, therefore, have an aversion to failure. The practice of avoiding failure in design can, however, discourage innovation and the rewards it brings. So, failure is an option, just ask Thomas Edison.

If we look at failure as an option at every step except in the final design (Slegers et al., 2012), failure is necessary for the design process as it allows us the opportunity to reassess the problem and the initial solutions. Since it is impossible to avoid failure, we can use it to reconsider the assumptions that we are making, the problem we have identified, the data we have collected and the process we are using. When failure is an option, we have an opportunity and a responsibility to learn from it. Failure is a common occurrence, and future success is based in part on our reaction to failure.

While failure gives us a chance to personally learn about our strengths and weaknesses, it may also trigger intense emotions (Fang He et al., 2018). In studying the degree to which entrepreneurs cope with and utilize their experiences with failure, researchers found that those who effectively controlled their emotions could positively learn from failure (Shepherd & Cardon, 2009). If, however, entrepreneurs had low or high rates of failure, they experienced difficulties learning from that failure. A moderate level of failing, one that was not too much or too little, balanced the negative emotions felt with the positive feelings of motivation. In other words, if they had a low failure rate, entrepreneurs remained content and lacked sufficient motivation to increase their learning from that failure. With a high failure rate, the negative emotions distracted entrepreneurs from engaging in learning from that failure. An intermediate level of failure rate, however, resulted in the highest level of learning behaviors.

Learning that it is OK to fail, and that failure is a normal part of the learning process also helps you learn important lessons about perseverance, determination, and effort. Through failure, you will get to know yourself better and you will learn from your mistakes. Failures make us rethink, reconsider, and find new ways and strategies to achieve our goals. As a designer cultivating your learning professional identity, remember IDEO's slogan regarding failure: "Fail often in order to succeed sooner" (Brown, 2009, p. 17).

How Do I Develop My Designer Learning Identity?

Your inborn characteristics and formal education have so far supported your designer learning journey, but this is only the beginning. Relying solely on the knowledge gained in formal education, especially as a designer, is not enough. Our design profession is developing at a rapid pace making it essential for you to continuously learn, thus the need to develop your designer learning identity. Where do you begin? Begin by embracing the idea that you are responsible for your continuous learning. As a design professional taking responsibility to be an ongoing active learner includes asking questions, analyzing, and evaluating designs, and through practical experience.

Asking Questions

Learning how to ask questions may seem like an easy task, but to learn on a deep level, asking intelligent questions is not as simple as you may think. If you do all the talking, you cut off gaining information from the very people you need to learn from. So, be curious and direct, listen more, and talk less. Ask open-ended questions that help people reveal what they are thinking and why they think in a particular way. Open-ended questions also prevent you from making judgments based on your assumptions.

Sakichi Toyoda, the founder of the Toyota automobile company created a process called the 5Ys (Harrington & Voehl, 2016) initially used in manufacturing. In its basic form, you begin the process of asking *why* five times until you get past all the symptoms of a problem and down to the root cause. You may ask more or fewer *whys,* depending on the information you want to learn. This open-ended question process is not only a powerful assessment method, but also a simple way to uncover problems that are not clear or obvious. As a designer, you can use this technique as a tool to discover new information and develop your learning identity.

Using *what*, *how*, and *why* questions to encourage dialogue also promotes learning. It isn't enough, however, to ask these open-ended questions; you must be engaged in listening to the responses. Showing that you are interested and using whatever means you prefer to document and remember the information, be it through writing, sketching, and/or recording the exchange, indicates your engagement. Being engaged shows the person you are talking with that you are interested in learning what they have to say and what they can teach you. Ask for clarification and dig deeper to make sure you avoid the mistake of assuming you have learned all the information you need. Do not be afraid to dig for details and get the whole story. There is so much to learn when you listen to someone's personal stories. Asking someone to tell you the story is one way you can learn and understand design problems that others may find hard to describe. Asking open-ended questions allows you to gather the information needed to critically analyze and evaluate other designs.

Analyzing and Evaluating Designs

Analyzing and evaluating other designs increases your design knowledge and cultivates your designer learning identity. Use your skill of asking questions to critique and evaluate existing and past designs. Question the design by reflecting if you believe it is good or bad, correct or incorrect, effective or ineffective, relevant or irrelevant to the context designed for and why? Reflect on the advantages and disadvantages of the design, and if you believe it is the best solution to a problem or issue. What do you like about the design and what would you change? Then, go a step further and articulate why you answered these questions the way you did.

The aim of ongoing learning in design is to develop you as a professional who can tackle any problem by drawing on your design knowledge. By continuously looking at and critiquing other designers' products, your design knowledge continues to grow. Everything man made has been designed by someone so don't limit yourself to studying products only in your design field. Why does your coffee pot look and work the way it does? How does the exercise equipment you use meet your needs? What is it about your favorite outfit and pair of shoes that makes them something you love to wear? Through focused analysis and evaluation of other designs, you develop your critical and analytic thinking skills (Nelsons & Stolterman, 2012). Each time you critique a design, you advance your ability to assess the features, usefulness, and appearance of designs. You also expand your understanding of the design process and the elements of a successful design.

Learning from Practical Experience

Every time you engage in some form of design, you learn. By being open to all design activities, you will continue to gain practical experience to support your designer learning identity. Think about your best designs thus far, then think about your design failures. What did you learn from each of these design experiences? We have touched on the need to continuously engage in design activity to cultivate your professional designer identity in other segments (see: Collaboration and Communication), but here we want to focus on how you can learn from your design activity by reflecting on the design process, the design product and with other designers (see Collaboration). When engaging in a design project, take a few moments at the end of every day to reflect on what surprised you, what was the most important thing you learned, where do you want to start tomorrow, and what will you do differently. What worked in your design process today and what didn't work? When were you creative and when did you stumble? What do you like about your design and what still needs work? By reflecting daily on the design process and the product you are creating, you gain new knowledge about design while you are designing. Documenting your answers and then asking these questions to others on the design team promotes your reflection ability and your ongoing designer knowledge.

Keep your reflection notes along with an updated portfolio of your designs to continuously refer to and reflect on your designer knowledge growth. Your portfolio can consist of ideas, successes, failures, reflections, and examples of your designs. You may find inspirations from music, nature, art, or literature that you want to include in your portfolio. Since it has been shown that when creating an ePortfolio as a learning activity, students developed self-regulated learning (de Bont & Liu, 2017), having an ongoing portfolio is an excellent way of cultivating your designer learning identity. The process of creating and maintaining a portfolio supports skill development by encouraging reflective thinking, helping designers recognize their strengths and limitations, and in improving their methods of learning (Romero et al., 2019). So, learning from practical experience includes participating in design activities, reflecting and documenting your ongoing design process and products, and creating and maintaining a portfolio of your ideas and designs.

Continuous learning supports your designer learning identity – your partner as you travel down the road of cultivating your designer professional identity.

We have kept you in suspense long enough. What was it that Makayla learned from a playground kickball game and her high school days as a shortstop that helped her team design an intervention for the company's leaders? First off, Makayla remembered Coach Jackson and her love of James P. Carse's book – *Finite and Infinite Games*. During that magical softball season, Coach Jackson would share ideas from *Finite and Infinite Games*. Coach Jackson would stress that the team had to be prepared *for* surprise, not prepared *against* surprise. That is what it means to be a smart softball player who is ready for any situation. While watching, the kickballers use a lunch box for first base, a piece of cardboard for second base, and a balled-up sweatshirt for third base, Makayla smiled and thought of another Coach Jackson-ism. A championship team plays *with* boundaries while other teams play *within* boundaries. When a team understands that a game's dynamics change each inning, then the team plays to the surprises that happen with each pitch. As Makayla hustled back to the office, her design ideas were flourishing.

Takeaways

- Designers learn from education and experience, from practice and observation, from success and failure.
- Design by its very nature is learning so you learn through design.
- Previous life experience is the basis for new learning.
- Experiential learning through concrete, reflect, abstract, and activate actions, promotes continuous learning.
- Learning from design practice and through design projects are important ways to learn from design.
- Learning from failure is an opportunity for personal and professional growth.
- Failure is an option at every design step except in the final design.
- Develop your designer learning identity by asking questions, analyzing/evaluating designs, and from practical design experience.

Exercises to Develop Your Designer Learning

1. **Memory lane**: Reflective writing is one way to help you recognize moments in your life that were important learning lessons. Take out your design journal and reflect on and answer one or more of these prompts:
   - What was my favorite class in grade school and why was it my favorite?
   - What lessons in my life play over and over in my brain today and why?
   - Who are some of my favorite artists (musical, visual, performing etc.) and why?
   - What lessons did I learn from some of my favorite activities as a child?

2. **Design feedback**: Identify one design intervention you are currently working on or have completed. Sit down with someone you trust who has expertise in your design area. Take at least 45 minutes to ask your trusted colleague open-ended questions about your design and really listen to their responses. Questions can include:
   - What do you like and dislike with this design?
   - What advantages and disadvantages do you see in using this design?
   - What would you change in this design?
   - Who do you think will benefit from this design and why?

   After this exchange, take a moment along to reflect on these questions:
   - What did I learn about myself through this activity?
   - What did I learn about design through this activity?

3. **Current design reflection**: Think about a design intervention you are currently working on. At the end of one day of work, take your design journal and reflect on and answer the following prompts:
   - What did I learn today while designing?
   - How will I begin designing tomorrow because of what I learned today?
   - What did I do to help me during my design process today?

- What do I like about my current design?
- What still needs work in my current design and why?
- What will I do to improve my design?
- Who can I talk to about my design for help and support?

4. **Commit:** Commit to learning one new thing each and every day. It can be something personal, a fun fact, a new word, or a new design. Use your design journal every night to write down the one new thing you learned today and how it cultivates your designer professional identity.

Exercises for Designers Who Teach

1. **ePortfolio**: The purpose of this assignment is to have your students develop an ePortfolio which represents their design work completed over the course of their program. You can also have them add items such as ideas, reflections, and thoughts on other designs etc.

   Introduction: One of the key aspects to design is building your personal brand to showcase your skills, experience, accomplishments, and interests for future employers. Your ePortfolio is representative of the work you have created in your educational program and in your life.

Tasks

- **Develop a website** to house artifacts and products from your classes
- **Create an About You/Bio section** which can include:
  - previous and current work experience
  - a design mantra or philosophy
  - skills, abilities, and marketable qualities
- You may choose to add products and projects that inspire you, that you find interesting, and that help you learn about design.

Energy for Your Journey

Educating the mind without educating the heart is no education at all.
(Aristotle)

References

Alhajri, S. (2016). The effectiveness of teaching methods used in graphic design peda-gogy in both analogue and digital education systems. *Universal Journal of Education-al Research, 4*(2), 422–425. doi: https://doi.org/10.13189/ujer.2016.040216

Brown, T. (2009). *Change by design: How design thinking transforms organizations and inspires innovation.* HarperCollins.

Cross, N. (2011). *Design thinking: Understanding how designers think and work.* Berg.

de Bont, C., & Liu, S. X. (2017). Breakthrough innovation through design education: Perspectives of design-led innovators. *Design Issues, 33*(2), 18–30. doi: https://doi.org/10.1162/DESI_a_00437

Dorst, K. (2003). *Understanding design: 150 reflections on being a designer.* Bis Publishers.

Fang He, V., Sirén, C., Singh, S., Solomon, G., & von Krogh, G. (2018). Keep calm and carry on: Emotion regulation in entrepreneurs' learning from fail-ure. *Entrepreneurship Theory and Practice, 42*(4), 605–630. doi: https://doi.org/10.1177/1042258718783428

Harrington, H. J., & Voehl, F. (Eds.). (2016). *The innovation tools handbook, volume 2: Evolutionary and improvement tools that every innovator must know* (1st ed.). Produc-tivity Press.

Isaacson, W. (2011). *Steve jobs.* Simon & Schuster.

Kolb, D. A., & Fry, R. E. (1975). *Toward an applied theory of experiential learning: Theories of group processes.* John Wiley & Sons.

Lave, J., & Wenger, E. (1991). *Situated learning: Legitimate peripheral participation.* Cambridge University Press.

Lawson, B., & Dorst, K. (2009). *Design expertise* (1st ed.). Routledge.

Nelsons, H. G., & Stolterman, E. (2012). *The design way: Intentional change in an unpre-dictable world* (2nd ed.). The MIT Press.

Romero, L., Saucedo, C., Caliusco, M. L., & Gutiérrez, M. (2019). Supporting self-regulated learning and personalization using ePortfolios: A semantic approach based on learning paths. *International Journal of Educational Technology in Higher Education, 16*(1), 1–16. doi: https://doi.org/10.1186/s41239-019-0146-1

Shepherd, D. A., & Cardon, M. S. (2009). Negative emotional reactions to project fail-ure and the self-compassion to learn from the experience. *Journal of Management Studies, 46*(6), 923–949. doi: https://doi.org/10.1111/j.1467-6486.2009.00821.x

Slegers, N. J., Kadish, R. T., Payton, G. E., Thomas, J., Griffin, M. D., & Dumbacher, D. (2012). Learning from failure in systems engineering: A panel discussion. *Sys-tems Engineering, 15*(1), 74–82. doi: https://doi.org/10.1002/sys.20195

Yang, M.-Y., You, M., & Chen, F.-C. (2005). Competencies and qualifications for industrial design jobs: Implications for design practice, education, and student career guidance. *Design Studies, 26*(2), 155–189. doi: https://doi.org/10.1016/j.destud.2004.09.003

COMMUNICATION

Working with oncologists, Makayla had an opportunity to design a one-hour online course to guide general physician practitioners on how to treat patients post cancer. Meeting with the expert oncologists, Makayla quickly realized they were speaking a different language than she was accustomed to. Sitting with the four cancer specialists, two nurses, and a medical office manager, Makayla was struck by how little she understood the information they were providing. She was also having a difficult time conveying her design ideas for the online course. Makayla thought "we have to find a better way to communicate with each other."

Communication in design is an interchange with those involved in the design giving, receiving and/or exchanging ideas, information, and messages.

Welcome to communication. Fold your journey map to this stop and get ready to cultivate your designer communication professional identity. Design is not an isolated activity, so communication is an essential

DOI: 10.4324/9781003255154-9

element in your designer development journey. Like Makayla, you will continuously interact with individuals whose information you need and who you must exchange ideas with, in an effort to successfully design. The way you communicate with others and present your ideas makes a lasting impression on people and will ultimately impact your innovative design ability.

What Is Communication in Design?

Did you ever play the *telephone* game as a child? In the game, players sit in a circle; one player whispers a sentence to the next player, who nods that they heard it, then whispers it to the next player and so on until the last player hears the sentence and recites it out loud. The first player then tells the rest of the group the initial sentence, for all to hear how much the sentence changed as it was passed from one player to the next. This is one example of communication, a form of conveying information or messages from one person or place to another. This is also an example of how easy it is to have a communication failure while transferring that information or message. The *telephone* game players are engaged in a two-way communication process using the following basic elements: a *sender* (the player who provides the initial sentence), a *message* (the sentence), a *channel* (verbal whispering), and a *receiver* (the other players), all part of the communication process (Richey et al., 2011). These elements also apply to three forms of communication that impact designers, verbal, non-verbal, and visual. Let's take a brief look at each of these forms of communication.

Verbal Communication

Verbal communication, speaking through language, is the most common form of communication. Have you ever been with a child before they are able to talk? Although they do not have formal language abilities yet, they verbally communicate through crying, coos, laughing, and other sounds. Once able to use language, the child recognizes that language is one of the most important tools of communication. In design, verbal communication "is a social process, as an effort to establish a 'commonness' with someone" (Gerbner as cited in Richey et al., 2011, p.36). In this social process, the *sender* (you as the designer) and the *receiver* (other designers, clients etc.) work in unison to share information, ideas, or attitudes with each person interpreting the *messages* they are sending and receiving. This verbal social process is constant, dynamic, and includes *feedback* from you as the designer, other designers, clients, and stakeholders, as everyone involved attempts to understand the *messages* and come to agreement. There are multiple *channels* you can use when verbally communicating, such as phones, Internet calling tools, and social networking sites. In addition to in-person gatherings, there are numerous video and web conferencing tools you can use to communicate. The *messages* you engage in may include asking questions, sharing stories, verbally confirming the accuracy of information you have heard, and providing design ideas to your fellow design team members and clients. Verbal communication, however, is not the only social form of communication, let's take a brief look at nonverbal communication.

Nonverbal Communication

Have you ever shared a story about a difficult moment in your life with someone and watched how their body reacted as you spoke? Were they looking right at you, nodding their head, crossing their arms, or moving their bodies? Although you were the person speaking, they were using nonverbal communication, the sharing of information by way of body language such as facial expressions, body movements and posture, listening, and eye contact. Now, think about the reaction you wanted from the person listening to your difficult story. When you are the person listening, it is important for you as the *sender* to show that you are actively listening by maintaining eye contact, nodding your head, and giving the *receiver* your undivided attention. We know that the human face and body is an extremely expressive *channel* and able to communicate numerous *messages* without saying a single word. This is the power of nonverbal communication. Listening is one of the key *messages* you can employ when participating in effective nonverbal communication. When you let others talk while maintaining eye contact and paying attention, you are communicating to the *receiver* that you are engaged and giving them your undivided attention. So nonverbal communication sends *messages* from the *sender* to the *receiver* using actions rather than words. There are multiple *channels* you can use when sending *messages* through nonverbal communication such as using hand gestures, eye contact, body language, and facial expressions.

Visual Communication

Think back to a moment you were emotionally moved by a letter, photo, or story from a loved one. Has a fellow designer ever shown you their design idea in a sketch that triggered another idea? These are examples of visual communication, sharing information in written forms, symbols, numbers, and/or sketches. Visual communication is the most important form of communication for you as a designer. Sketching is a method where you can thoughtfully and mindfully engage in the design process and communicate your ideas. Through sketching not only do you as the *sender* convey your design ideas to the *receiver,* you also can use this *channel* of visual communication to expand, refine, and evaluate your design. The best designers are those who sketch, because when you sketch as your means of communicating you may be *sending* your design ideas verbally, non-verbally, and visually to your *receiver(s)*. The use of multiple *channels* to convey your message will increase the possibility of shared understanding between all involved in the design. There are other *channels* you can use when sending *messages* through visual communication such as photography, drawing, charts and graphs, mail, email, and SMS/text messaging.

It is important, however, to remember that all three of these forms of communication will be *sent* and *received* differently based on culture, age, gender, and geographic location. A design team designing instruction in the United Arab Emirates (U.A.E.) learned that visually sketching the entire body to illustrate certain work functions was culturally inappropriate for their audience. As a result, all sketched images were of the hands only. As a designer, it is crucial to understand the *receivers* of your *messages,* because using suitable *channels* to send your *messages* will increase the outcome of a successful design.

As a designer, it is critical for you to communicate effectively on a personal and interpersonal level. Your interpersonal communication professional identity includes your ability to establish rapport, collaborate, engage in public presentations, and communicate among a team.

Your personal communication professional identity includes your ability to communicate clearly, directly, and empathize with your audience.

How Does Listening Relate to Communication?

When communicating with others, we often focus on what we should do or say. However, effective communication in design is less about talking and more about listening. Listening is the ability to accurately receive and understand messages when you are engaged in verbal, non-verbal, and visual communication (Wolvin, 2010). Therefore, the most effective communication skill you can have when developing your designer professional identity is becoming an observant listener. Without the ability to listen effectively, messages are easily misunderstood, so listening is the primary way to develop relationships, understand others, and build trust. To listen, you need to make a conscious effort not just to hear what people are saying but to take it in, digest it, and understand it. Active listening, for you as a designer, means paying close attention to who you're communicating with by engaging with them, asking questions, and rephrasing. It is critical when listening to another person to remember that it's not about you, but about the person you are communicating with. So, listening not only enhances your ability to understand better, but it also makes the experience of speaking to you more enjoyable to other people. Since design is not an isolated activity, as a designer who really listens, you will improve the continuous communication process you are in, exchanging ideas and achieving a mutual understanding with all of those involved in your design.

How Do I Communicate in a Design Team?

A cross-cultural design team designing an instructional intervention to train workers on how to clean the largest mall in the world realized they each called the washroom something different. Those from Europe called it the water closet or WC, those from the U.S.A. called it the bathroom or restroom, while some from the U.A.E. called it the Loo. Although English was the common language on the design team, they soon discovered that terms for common items were one of the many communication challenges they had. To solve this challenge, the team created a written list of agreed upon terms to use for the hundreds of items that needed to be identified to complete this large-scale design project. This negotiated team solution was only achieved through the collective group communication process.

Communication is a social process fundamental to design work (Alexiou et al., 2009). When working in a design team, communication is performed by team members situated in a rich and dynamic social context (Ball et al., 2004). Innovative design depends on how well a team communicates with each other. How do you as a designer communicate in a design team? There are numerous communication functions you and the members of your design team ought to identify and agree upon to engage in productive team communication. Here are three essential tools to consider.

Shared Commitment

An interdisciplinary design team worked collaboratively to design an intensive week-long certification course on integrating biology, radio oncology, and physics for medical personnel (Tracey, 2015). Although each member of the team came from a different place with unique experiences, values, and beliefs, the team had a common goal and made decisions, shared resources, and responsibilities to achieve that goal. Working together for five years, the team never fully understood each other's professions, but this did not prevent them from creating a shared commitment where all members agreed on a common purpose to reach their design goal. Their shared commitment began with a shared understanding. The team met weekly for two hours, face-to-face, which positively influenced the initial creation of a shared understanding (Kleinsmann & Valkenburg, 2008). When not in face-to-face meetings, the team met virtually using drawings and prototypes to build a shared understanding of the design between each team member. It was the ongoing verbal, non-verbal, and visual communication that assisted this unique interdisciplinary team in creating and maintaining their shared commitment over five years.

One of the tools the design team used to gain a shared understanding and ultimately shared commitment was a design frame (Dorst, 2003), a process where the team agreed on how to "frame" the problem and determine the direction to follow. Design frames may include identifying artificial or actual constraints on the design, listing all the elements of the problem, or identifying the items the problem does not contain. For this design team, some of the constraints included choosing content and strategies to teach three very different disciplines how to collaborate for patient care in only five days. The team had pages of identified elements of this problem and had to come to a shared understanding and commitment of the final solution. This was one of the communication tools used to assist the design team in creating and maintaining a shared commitment. A shared commitment is essential for constructive design team communication.

Sense of Community

You are a member of the extensive design community, and as a member of a design team, you become a member of a smaller design community. When each team member has a sense of belonging, the team develops a sense of community. How do you create a sense of belonging for yourself and your team members? As a designer with a strong communication professional identity, you can create friendly communication with other team members to help build a sense of community. Begin to get to know your team members through casual social activities, informal "getting to know you" social meetings, and/or organized team-building events. Having face-to-face meetings/activities, especially before the design project begins, can encourage closer bonding, build a sense of community, and help to prevent misunderstandings and minimize conflict once the team is established. These social interactions before the actual teamwork begins encourages interpersonal relationships which support the development of professional identity (Blouin, 2018).

Once design team sessions begin, continue to create opportunities for you and your team members to build and strengthen the sense of community. Engaging in activities such as virtual shared coffee breaks to catch up on nonwork issues may help keep the social bonds within the team alive. One virtual design team organized a 15-minute "sharing session" prior to each scheduled design team meeting where members shared personal updates, interesting photos, and/or stories. These actions can help team members develop a sense of belonging, strengthen relationships, and build a sense of community.

As a designer with a strong communication professional identity, you can cultivate a sense of team community by making sure all members can verbally share information, ask questions, and are receptive to what others in your team are contributing. Your nonverbal communication skills (i.e., eye contact, active listening, and positive body language) can foster a sense of community with your team. A sense of belonging on a design team means all members are heard, have an opportunity to contribute, and are aware of what other members are thinking and doing. Transparency of the design process builds a sense of community.

Communication Style

The cross-cultural design team designing the instructional intervention to train workers how to clean the largest mall in the world realized that in the design solution, written words were not possible when teaching the over 400 laborers, who all spoke different languages. Additionally, each design team member brought their own communication style to the team, and all had different ideas how to proceed. It was crucial that the team create a common language to talk about the design. This became a balancing act as the team realized they needed a truly unique design and having concrete concepts too soon might prevent them from creating the most innovative solution possible. The team initially talked about the design by creating a communication style using three words: *color, pictures, and symbols.* They agreed that these were the means they would use to design the instructional intervention but wanted to maintain a creative space for how to use these means for innovative design ideas to emerge. No one outside of the design team understood the team meanings of these words. The design team established its own communication style.

We know that design is fluid so in the beginning, the language may consist of drawings, sketches, abbreviated words, such as the example above or vague design terms. This initial communication style, also called *DesignSpeak*, needs to remain vague and fluid for the team to avoid "freezing" the image of what the design could be too soon (Dorst, 2003). In developing your design team's communication style use language, an important tool in design, carefully. For the cross-cultural design team, the meaning of the words *color, pictures,* and *symbols,* referring to the design, changed dramatically during the life of the design project. Their meaning developed from ambiguous to specific with each word taking on a completely different meaning by the end of the design. In this design team, these words were referred to in shorthand. As a result, the design team developed its own subculture foreign to the outside world and to new team members. As the project expanded and other designers joined the team, current members had to indoctrinate new members on the team's communication style. This was critical as different interpretations had to be prevented especially as the design project came close to completion.

How Do I Cultivate My Designer Communication?

Your ability to communicate directly impacts the growth of your designer professional identity since professional identity and communication play a reciprocal role in your designer professional identity development. The communication abilities you develop (Holmes, 2006) will reinforce (Hatmaker, 2013; Leisti-Szymczak et al., 2013) your professional identity development (Apker & Eggly, 2004; Shakespeare & Webb, 2008; Vågan, 2009). Additionally, a strong sense of your designer professional identity will reinforce your communication skills and your confidence (Blouin, 2018; Kremer-Hayon et al., 2002; Vågan, 2009). In other words, the more you develop your designer communication skills, the more you will develop your designer professional identity, and the more you develop your professional identity, the more you will develop your designer communication skills.

One of the ways to do this is to gain experience by engaging in the practice of design. The most used tool to help you as a designer develop interpersonal skills and professional identity is direct experience with the types of interactions you can expect as a practicing professional (Binyamin, 2018; Plack, 2006; Shakespeare & Webb, 2008; Vågan, 2009). These experiences will provide you with the opportunity to practice your communication skills while you handle design challenges and interactions with team members, clients, and the audience of focus, in your professional designer role. If you are not currently working as a practicing designer, this may be difficult but not impossible. Taking all the strategies from this communication segment, (engaging in verbal, non-verbal, and visual communication, working in a team to develop a shared commitment, sense of community, and communication style), find a place you can volunteer to practice your design skills. Are you a member of a community or school group, a religious organization or a non-profit? These organizations will often have a need for something to be designed but will not have the funds to do so. Create an opportunity for you and your design community to practice and develop your designer communication skills while designing a solution for a worthy cause. This will help you accumulate expertise and skills.

Do you communicate in a current design community or have a professional network? Your designer social abilities, demonstrated through communication, will assist your communication professional identity development through expanding your expertise and skills (Cohen-Scali, 2003), and by creating a professional network (Dobrow & Higgins, 2005). Gaining experience, through professional job opportunities and volunteer design opportunities such as the ones mentioned above will help you accumulate your design expertise and allow you to meet fellow designers to grow your professional network. But this is not the only way to create your designer community. Find local, regional, and national design organizations, even if they are different from your design field. You are a designer first after all, who designs in a specific area, but as a designer, engaging with other designers in the large design community will help you develop your social abilities. Your professional network impacts your capacity to establish a designer professional identity, and the ability to establish a professional network relies on your interpersonal skills (Baer, 2012; Binyamin, 2018; Blouin, 2018; Park et al., 2018). So, developing your communication skills will help you develop your interpersonal skills which will grow your professional network, which will help you cultivate your professional identity.

Takeaways

- Communication in design is a social process fundamental to design work.
- The three basic forms of communication in design are verbal, nonverbal, and visual.
- Designers communicate on a personal and interpersonal level.

- Effective communication in design is less about talking and more about listening.
- Three essential communication functions for productive design team communication are: a shared commitment, a sense of community, and a communication style.
- The more you develop your designer communication skills, the more you will develop your designer professional identity, and the more you develop your professional identity, the more you will develop your designer communication skills.
- Design experience and a professional network builds your designer social abilities and your communication professional identity.

Exercises to Cultivate My Designer Communication

1. **This is what I do:**

   It is often difficult to communicate your design work/profession so that a person unfamiliar with your work has a clear picture of what you do.
   - In 10 minutes, write down a clear description of what you do in design.
   - It cannot include the word "design" or the name of the design field you are in. As an example, it cannot include the words graphic design or engineering design.
   - Think about the person/people you will be communicating what you do to, making sure they do not have any prior awareness of what you do. How should you communicate your profession to them? What words and descriptions will help them clearly understand what you do?
   - Set a timer and write your brief clear description of what you do.
   - When the 10 minutes are up, call or physically meet a person to share your description.
   - After you read it, ask them to describe what you do. Were they accurate? What can you do to improve how you communicate what you do to others?

2. **Listening.... and talking:**

For this activity, you will need a partner. Invite a family member, friend or colleague to engage in this short 10-minute activity. Using the topic below, it is time to listen and talk.

- Sit across from each other and set a timer for 3 minutes. Let your partner go first.
- For 3 minutes, listen… do not talk while the other person is talking. Be sure to pay attention and to look directly at the speaker.
- Be aware of listening to the other person when he or she is talking instead of preparing for your turn.
- Make sure you are paying attention to how the person is behaving. Be aware of the body language of the other person.
- Let the other person know that you are listening – eye contact, nodding your head, etc.
- When the other person stops talking, try to paraphrase or translate what he or she said. Reflect what you think you have heard.
- Now, have the other person talk, repeating all of the steps above.

The Topic:

- Describe a time when you failed at something.
- How did you feel?
- What did you do?
- What did you learn about yourself?
- If you could go back and talk to your younger self about this failure, what would you say?

3. **Draw your story**

Drawing and sketching are the most important communication tools for a designer. Get a large piece of paper, markers, colored pencils, etc., and settle for this quiet visual activity. Take as much time as you need to reflect on your life and the events that led you to where and who you are today. Now… draw your story.

- Begin in the beginning, your childhood, what illustrations best describe the first 10 years of your life? What were you like, what did you do, and how did you feel during your early years? How can you capture that in this drawing?

- Next, move onto your teen age years, what drawings will best describe these years? What were your highlights, difficult times, and instances of intense growth?
- Finally, enter adulthood with your sketch. What visuals do you want to convey to best describe the events of your adulthood? Do you include other people in your depictions, major events, and/or interesting places you have gone?
- When you are finished, look carefully and closely at your illustration. Do you describe your story clearly? Can you feel the emotions you felt during these years in your drawing? If you are willing, share it with someone who has known you since childhood and ask them to describe what they see. Do they communicate what you were trying to convey? Does your illustration describe your story?

4. **Engage in practice**
   - One of the best ways to develop your communication designer professional identity is to engage in practice. If you are currently working in the design field with a design team, you can engage in practice applying all the communication tools in this segment.
   - If you are not yet working in your design field, you can still engage in practice.
   - Make a list of all the organizations you are currently a member of, a place of worship or religious organization, your school or community groups, non-profit organizations you or people you know are members of such as the animal shelter, soup kitchens, or homeless shelters.
   - Narrow the list to three organizations where you have or can get a contact person to reach out to.
   - Reach out to the contact person and set up a meeting to discuss some of their design challenges. Volunteer to help the organization solve one of their design problems. Choose one that you know you can successfully complete with the time and expertise you have.
   - If you can engage with other designers to form a design team, that is ideal. All design work, whether part of a team

or as an individual, should be done in communication with the audience of focus, the client, and any other stakeholders while you design.

- Make sure to use all of the communication tools in this segment to successfully design a solution for your nonprofit organization.

5. **Develop your network**

- One way to develop your social ability and your interpersonal skills is to develop and engage with a designer professional network.

- Conduct a search of the professional design organizations in your area. Visit each organization's website to learn about what they do and who their members are.

- Choose one design organization that fits into your current life situation. Can you attend the meetings? Can you afford the membership? Is their mission and vision something you are interested in?

- Join the organization and make a commitment to be an active member for one year. Attend the meetings with the goal of establishing one new designer as a contact from every meeting. If you attend one meeting a month, by the end of the year you will have a designer professional network that includes 12 additional designers.

Exercises for Designers Who Teach

1. **Back-to-back drawing**

- Prepare a set of simple illustrations, they can be geometric images, simple drawings, or pictures.

- Have all of your designer participants partner off and sit-back-to-back with a paper and pencil each. Have each partner group select one person to be speaker and one person to be listener.

- Once decided, pass out one illustration to each speaker in the partnership making sure the listener does not see it.

- Over five to ten minutes, the speaker describes the illustration, and the listener tries to replicate this illustration without looking at the image. The listener cannot ask any questions or seek clarification. They must only listen.

- When time is up, have the listener and the speaker put the two illustrations side by side.
- Bring all the designer participants back together and as a group, have volunteers talk about the experience, using several of the following example questions:

2. **Speaker questions**
   - What steps did you take to ensure your instructions were clear?
   - What challenges did you have communicating how your listener needed to draw the illustration?
   - While speaking, what could you have done to decrease the chance of miscommunication?

3. **Listener questions**
   - What was constructive about your partner's instructions?
   - What was challenging about your partner's instructions?
   - In what ways might your drawing have turned out differently if you could have communicated with your partner?

Energy for Your Journey

If you just communicate you can get by. But if you communicate skillfully, you can work miracles.

Jim Rohn (Jones, 2019)

Are you a skillful design communicator?

References

Alexiou, K., Zamenopoulos, T., Johnson, J. H., & Gilbert, S. J. (2009). Exploring the neurological basis of design cognition using brain imaging: Some preliminary results. *Design Studies, 30*(6), 623–647. doi: https://doi.org/10.1016/j.destud.2009.05.002

Apker, J., & Eggly, S. (2004). Communicating professional identity in medical socialization: Considering the ideological discourse of morning report. *Qualitative Health Research, 14*(3), 411–429. doi: https://doi.org/10.1177/1049732303260577

Baer, M. (2012). Putting creativity to work: The implementation of creative ideas in organizations. *The Academy of Management Journal*, 55(5), 1102–1119. https://www.jstor.org/stable/23412455%0A

Ball, L. J., Ormerod, T. C., & Morley, N. J. (2004). Spontaneous analogising in engineering design: A comparative analysis of experts and novices. *Design Studies*, 25(5), 495–508. doi: https://doi.org/10.1016/j.destud.2004.05.004

Binyamin, G. (2018). Growing from dilemmas: Developing a professional identity through collaborative reflections on relational dilemmas. *Advances in Health Sciences Education*, 23(1), 43–60. doi: https://doi.org/10.1007/s10459-017-9773-2

Blouin, D. (2018). Impact of interpersonal relations on learning and development of professional identity: A study of residents' perceptions. *Emergency Medicine Australasia*, 30(3), 398–405. doi: https://doi.org/10.1111/1742-6723.12944

Cohen-Scali, V. (2003). The influence of family, social, and work socialization on the construction of the professional identity of young adults. *Journal of Career Development*, 29(4), 237–249. doi: https://doi.org/10.1177/089484530302900402.

Dobrow, S. R., & Higgins, M. C. (2005). Developmental networks and professional identity: A longitudinal study. *Career Development International*, 10(6/7), 567–583. doi: https://doi.org/10.1108/13620430510620629

Dorst, K. (2003). *Understanding design: 150 reflections on being a designer.* Bis Publishers.

Hatmaker, D. M. (2013). Engineering identity: Gender and professional identity negotiation among women engineers. *Gender, Work & Organization*, 20(4), 382–396. doi: https://doi.org/10.1111/j.1468-0432.2012.00589.x

Holmes, J. (2006). Workplace narratives, professional identity and relational practice. In A. De Fina, D. Schiffrin, & M. Bamberg (Eds.), *Discourse and identity* (pp. 166–187). Cambridge University Press. doi: https://doi.org/10.1017/CBO9780511584459.009

Kleinsmann, M., & Valkenburg, R. (2008). Barriers and enablers for creating shared understanding in co-design projects. *Design Studies*, 29(4), 369–386. doi: https://doi.org/10.1016/j.destud.2008.03.003

Kremer-Hayon, L., Faraj, H., & Wubbels, T. (2002). Burn-out among Israeli Arab school principals as a function of professional identity and interpersonal relationships with teachers. *International Journal of Leadership in Education*, 5(2), 149–162. doi: https://doi.org/10.1080/13603120110057091

Leisti-Szymczak, A., Liikkanen, L. A., Laakso, M., & Summanen, I. (2013). Let me do my job – Industrial designer's experiences of client collaboration. *Proceedings of CO-CREATE 2013 - The Boundary-Crossing Conference on Co-Design in Innovation*, 445–456.

Park, J. J., Chuang, Y. C., & Hald, E. S. (2018). Identifying key influencers of professional identity development of Asian international STEM graduate students in the United States. *Asia-Pacific Education Researcher*, 27(2), 145–154. doi: https://doi.org/10.1007/s40299-018-0373-6

Plack, M. M. (2006). The development of communication skills, interpersonal skills, and a professional identity within a community of practice. *Journal of Physical Therapy Education*, 20(1), 37–46. doi: https://doi.org/10.1097/00001416-200601000-00005

Richey, R., Klein, J. D., & Tracey, M. W. (2011). *The instructional design knowledge base: Theory, research, and practice.* Routledge.

Jones, M. (2019, April 25). *Saying it right: How to enhance communication in the workplace.* Vocovo. https://www.vocovo.com/blog/post/saying-it-right-how-to-enhance-communication-in-the-workplace/

Shakespeare, P., & Webb, C. (2008). Professional identity as a resource for talk: Exploring the mentor-student relationship. *Nursing Inquiry*, 15(4), 270–279. doi: https://doi.org/10.1111/j.1440-1800.2008.00415.x

Tracey, M. W. (2015). Design team collaboration with a complex design problem. In B. Hokanson, G. Clinton, & M. W. Tracey (Eds.), *The design of learning experience. Educational communications and technology: Issues and innovations* (pp. 93–108). Springer. doi: https://doi.org/10.1007/978-3-319-16504-2_7

Vågan, A. (2009). Medical students' perceptions of identity in communication skills training: A qualitative study. *Medical Education, 43*(3), 254–259. doi: https://doi.org/10.1111/j.1365-2923.2008.03278.x

Wolvin, A. D. (Ed.) (2010). *Listening and human communication in the 21st century.* Wiley-Blackwell. doi: https://doi.org/10.1002/9781444314908

COLLABORATION

Makayla was part of a design team hired by a large educational company to create an intervention teaching math ratio concepts to adult learners with literacy-related knowledge skill gaps preparing to take their high school equivalency exam. In speaking with adult basic educators (ABEs) at the company, the ABEs stressed that adults who lack basic math skills perform better when they relate the math skill to their everyday lives. Makayla and some teammates were thrilled as they had extremely strong math backgrounds, one member had even been a high school math teacher. They could not wait to share their math expertise in the design for their audience of focus. Others on the team, however, identified themselves as math haters who wanted to design a friendly engaging solution to reduce math anxiety for the audience of focus. The team, therefore, did not have a common goal for this design. In preparing to present the initial prototype to the client, the team fell into dissention as the math "lovers" designed a ratio formula they wanted to be taught while the rest designed a ratio activity using an everyday illustration of a cup of coffee, black, with milk and with milk and sugar. This activity made sense to the math haters, teaching ratios, 1/3, 2/3, and whole; although other team

DOI: 10.4324/9781003255154-10

members argued that it was too simple. The team presented both activities to the ABEs who were thrilled with the coffee activity. Makayla walked away realizing having a common goal in collaboration was essential, and without her teammates and their collaborative effort, she would have designed the wrong product for this client.

Design is a collaborative effort, but true collaboration only exists when there is a common goal.

What Is Collaboration?

Welcome to collaboration. Take a moment to reflect on your designer professional identity journey, thus, far. What other stops have you made? Do you recognize how your own professional identity is developing? Collaboration is a unique stop on your journey, as it is here that you will learn how your designer professional identity merges with others. You can see from reading Makayla's collaboration story that even with all her efforts to develop her designer professional identity, if she does not know how to collaborate with other designers, she will have a difficult time creating an impactful design product for her audience. Design is fundamentally a collaborative effort; the best design ideas often occur from a collaborative creative process rather than from a single designer (Lawson & Dorst, 2009). Think about your own design projects. Who is in the room with you? A script writer. A graphic designer. A programmer. A project manager. An engineer. Who else? Sharing ideas and working with others to achieve a design may seem simple, but this doesn't just happen as you saw with Makayla. Collaboration only occurs when two or more designers share their ideas and skills to complete a task, achieve a goal or create something new. Design is a social process (Dorst, 2003) and as a collaborative designer, you must interact with and consider others' ideas, skills, experiences, and opinions to truly collaborate. How do you identify if it is a true collaboration? Cooperation includes informal relationships that exist without a common goal, but collaboration only exists when there is a common goal (Constantino & Cho, 2015). A common goal is a key element to collaboration.

To be more responsive to its customers, a car company wanted dealership sales representatives to use social media to interact with potential customers. The design team, made up of a lead instructional manager, project manager, scriptwriter, graphic designer, online course builder, lead programmer, and company dealership subject matter expert, locked themselves in a room with wall-to-wall whiteboards. The first question they asked themselves was "what is the common goal of the online course?" Four colors of whiteboard markers later, the design team concluded that the common goal was to teach the dealership sales representatives how to respond to the different ways customers use social media. At this point, the design ideas burst open as the team designed customer personas each using social media in a different way to purchase a new vehicle. Only when the design team determined the common goal was the team able to begin designing.

Why Collaborate?

Why do we collaborate in design? Although you may prefer to design alone, collaborating nurtures relationships, inspires teams, and is a necessary design skill when working with ill-structured problems (Buchanan et al., 2013). It provides an opportunity for designers to work with each other and *with* stakeholders and the audience of focus instead of *for* them (Brown & Katz, 2011). Collaborative teams that included the client found that with the right mix of people they could address difficult challenges with greater agility and speed up decision-making. This is significant for project momentum and team focus (Steane et al., 2020).

Moving the design toward completion is the number one goal for design teams. Inclusive leaders (those eliciting ideas) and decisive leaders (those choosing discussion topics and making decisions) help collaborative design activities evolve (Tracey, 2015). In collaborative design, leaders are those who propose the vision of the design along with an enthusiastic description of what is possible. Leaders, therefore, can be identified, naturally emerge, and often change during the lifetime of a collaborative design team. In other words, a design team may have numerous leaders throughout the life of the design project. When a team is well balanced in their roles and manages their negotiation well (Cross, 2011), the time collaborating can be productive and creative where each person builds on the ideas of others. When design is happening collaboratively, in real time and among people who know and trust each other, design is easier (Brown & Katz, 2011).

We know, however, that design is all about constraints. Designers use collaboration to manage constraints throughout the design process. Constraints can initiate innovation, refinement, and improvement in the design (Cross, 2011). Collaboration can help design teams identify design constraints, elaborate on those constraints, and ultimately recast the constraints as opportunities (Tracey, 2015). Constraints are always present in design activities, but collaborative designers use those constraints to creatively improve design ideas.

Designers also use collaboration to build and rebuild prototypes to envision and refine solutions. Prototypes created during the design process can be used as an opportunity to gain consensus/clarity *or* to further refine the design (Tracey, 2015). Collaboration with prototyping can resolve questions regarding the feasibility of existing ideas in the design. Prototypes are also used to communicate design ideas with each other in the team and with those outside the team including your client and your audience of focus. As a design team's process is complex, with numerous levels of activity occurring at the same time (Cross, 2011), prototyping also provides a means of collaborating and communicating.

As poor communication can be one of the first symptoms (and causes) of poor team collaboration, creative collaborations must have effective communication. As a member of a design team, you will have to communicate with others in your team who may be from other disciplines (See Communication). To work well together, all team members need to share ideas, have an agreed upon approach toward the design work, and have a common goal like the dealership sales representative design team. Remember that each designer on your team will bring their own designer professional identity to the collaboration. The most successful teams are those who can adopt a communication style that minimizes threats to the individual professional identity of each team member while enhancing group identity (Jordan & Babrow, 2013). There are several ways and tools you can use to adopt a team communication style to promote team collaboration. Some find that a nonhierarchical group structure and communication process encourages equitable participation by all group members, which supports creative collaboration (Constantino & Cho, 2015). This more horizontal structure can create an environment that supports every team member's participation and reduces their reluctance to share ideas. In this collaborative structure, all team members have an opportunity to equally share responsibility, risk, and reward for the final design. Sticky notes are a material that can facilitate communication and design collaboration by enabling shared attention and promoting the variation of turn-taking (Ball et al., 2021). We know that design materials such as sketches, prototypes, and other visuals are important in design activity, and we now know they are good resources to promote and ensure collaboration. Visiting the communication segment in this book will help you cultivate your designer communication skills, which will also help you collaborate in a design team. Collaboration creates opportunities for knowledge sharing, encourages designers on the team to learn from each other, build on each other's ideas and work together to ultimately achieve the design goal.

How Does Collaboration Impact Creativity?

Three of the greatest rock and roll songs of all time are Smokey Robinson's My Girl, The Beach Boys' Good Vibrations, and The Eagles' Hotel California. Who wrote My Girl? Smokey Robinson *and* Robert White. How about Good Vibrations? Brian Wilson *and* Mike Love. Don Felder *and* Don Henley *and* Glenn Frey creatively collaborated on Hotel California. Big egos collaborating on some of the best songs ever written!

Think about how you felt the last time you created something on your own. Did you experience a huge sense of accomplishment? Were you proud of your work? Did you want to put your stamp on your work so that others would know it was you who created it? If it is difficult for you as a designer to collaborate with others because you fear you may lose your creative identity related to your work, you are not alone. When studying instructional designers, researchers discovered that resistance to collaborations particularly in areas of intellectual property may be partially explained by threats to their identity

(Schwier et al., 2004). In other words, designers thought their designer professional identity was threatened if they lost control over their creative intellectual ideas. While you are trying to cultivate your designer professional identity, you may have a natural reaction to hold onto your creative ideas as they are an output of your growth as a professional. This is a common reaction.

As college students in medicine learned more about practicing in their field, they experienced a decline in their desire to collaborate with others. As the students began to develop their professional identity, they experienced more insecurity in their role and, thus, attempted to reduce collaboration to protect their identity. This insecurity became more amplified as they progressed through their program, as students later in the program demonstrated less readiness to collaborate with others outside of their profession (Stull & Blue, 2016). Why do you think this happened? Shifting from an "individual operator" to a "team-oriented" professional identity mode was not only challenging but also contributed to a decline in their attitude toward their own professional identity (Stull & Blue, 2016). As students began to identify themselves in their profession, they wanted to protect that identity, and the one way they believed they could do so was to protect their individual creative ideas. The results of these studies are not surprising as a person's creative genius is central to who they are, so it is easy to understand how they may resist collaboration (Steen, 2013). However, when Brian Wilson's creative genius with a melody came together with Mike Love's creative genius with lyrics, the result was good vibrations that continues to stand the test of time.

The truth, however, is that the changing nature of professional design is moving out of the realm of an individualized craft and into a collaborative process (Zamberlan & Wilson, 2017). This means that an important way to cultivate the creative side of your professional identity is to collaborate with others. Through collaboration, you will recognize yourself as a professional, participate in a mutual exploration of diverse perspectives, recognize that there isn't a "right" way, there is "your" way, and understand that navigating relationship dilemmas is all a part of being a professional. By collaborating with others, you will be able to better preserve ambiguity and support every idea being considered equally. Collaboration stimulates creativity because when a creative event occurs, collaboration supports further generation of that creative event (Constantino & Cho, 2015). Individuals who collaborate display traits such as broad-mindedness, which is closely related to creativity in professional identity. A creative designer mindset is one that embraces collaboration to tackle different topics and work with people from different cultures, ideologies, or beliefs (Reilly et al., 2002).

Cooperative creativity does not happen on an individual level but is a process of joint idea generation (Steen, 2013). It increases the capacity to create by combining ideas with others collectively. Combined with other attributes that foster collaboration such as openness, cooperative creativity emphasizes another facet of designer creativity based on collective creative practice (Bowen et al., 2016). Creativity is fostered through collaboration and collaboration cultivates creativity. Visit the creativity segment in the book to learn more.

Will I Lose My Professional Identity if I Collaborate?

A "creative hero" is a person who is credited for solving the greatest design problems and creating the most innovative designs. When you hear the name Steve Jobs, do you think of him as a "creative hero?" Steve Jobs said, "Great things in business are never done by one person, they are done by a team of people" (Beahm, 2011, p. 156). Despite our practice of celebrating a singular creative hero, most innovative work is done collaboratively (Constantino & Cho, 2015). So, it is important to move away from the fantasy that the creative process has one "creative hero" and instead embrace the reality of creative collaboration.

Unfortunately, most formally educated designers are trained to be "creative heroes" rather than creative collaborators. It has been discovered that although training designers in a design studio with first-year design students working collaboratively with peer tutors best prepares them for the reality of collaborative creation, most design programs educate designers to be individual "creative heroes" (Zamberlan & Wilson, 2017). This results in a major tension between the creative individual work that designers are being prepared to do, and the reality of the collaborative work that will be expected of designers employed in their fields (Coulentianos et al., 2019). So, there is a disconnect between the designer identity as "creative hero" that is developed in formal education and the designer identity as collaborator that is required in the workplace. To best cultivate your designer professional identity, you need to be a collaborator instead of a "creative hero."

How Do I Cultivate My Designer Collaboration?

Design collaboration is not always an easy or intuitive activity. Collaboration in design requires intentional efforts to structure and support each designer to form relationships which support the common goal. How do we do that? What behaviors must you as a collaborative designer demonstrate? As a designer in a collaborative team, you should possess collaborative behaviors including expressing your ideas, listening, and negotiating (Brereton et al., 1996). We have stated that you bring your identity to collaborations and the ability (or inability) to integrate your identity with the design team. Team members' identities, therefore, significantly impact collaborative outcomes. When working in teams, you must find a balance between your individual identity and the team identity. The way that you and others on the team respond to collaborations may be influenced by your perceived external threats to your individual identity (Gal et al., 2014; Schwier et al., 2004). In some cases, the success of a team is closely tied to the team's ability to form a cohesive team identity (Du et al., 2016; Jacobs, 2017). In other cases, the ability to form a cohesive team identity is dependent on each collaborator's perceptions of the team as successful (Du et al., 2016). In other words, if all team members choose a cohesive team identity over their individual designer identity and see that choice as producing a successful team, the team identity has a stronger chance of forming and producing a successful collaborative design experience.

There are many behaviors you can exhibit that will help you integrate your identity with a design team. Here we highlight three of them. As you read about these behaviors, reflect on where you are today with each one: a beginner, intermediate, or an expert.

Trust

As a designer, there will be times when you must rely on others to complete design tasks to achieve the common goal. The behavior needed in these situations is applying trust. Trust is the degree to which each person feels they can depend on the other to do what they say they will do. Can you let go of a task and feel secure that someone else will complete it? Can you release control of an idea and let someone else develop it? These are examples of applying trust necessary when working on a collaborative design team. When you successfully apply trust, you and others on the team feel safe and accepted with each member feeling the security to express ideas, and concerns, leading to deeper connections and a greater understanding of other team members. Trust allows the team to grow in compassion, communication, and competency.

Respect

When design team members have a deep trust in one another, it is easier to develop the collaborative ability of respect, the second essential behavior. We show respect for fellow team members by actively listening when they are talking and remaining open-minded to their ideas. Demonstrating respect also means valuing the diversity of fellow team members. Respect is one of the most important aspects of successful collaborations in design teams because it involves being open to and accepting new, creative, and original ideas.

Willingness

How do you define willingness, the third key collaborative behavior? When it comes to designing and creating something new, collaboration means having the willingness to change to make things better. Willingness also means letting go of your ideas knowing they might not develop the way they would if you worked alone. There will always be healthy conflict on design teams, as things will not always go your way, but as a collaborative team member, you must be adaptable with a readiness to abandon your initial ideas and be ready to shift gears and make changes to achieve an original design. Willingness requires an open disposition and an eagerness and enthusiasm to create something greater than the sum of each individual designer. When you have a willingness to learn from your fellow team members, you are open to and seeking out new experiences, ideas, and information that allows you to continue to cultivate your designer ability.

You only exercise your collaborative designer professional identity skills when working with others, so seek opportunities to collaborate as often as possible. This is the only way you will cultivate these skills and develop your collaboration designer professional identity.

Takeaways: Collaboration

- Design is fundamentally a collaborative effort.
- True collaboration only exists when there is a common goal.
- Leaders can be identified, naturally emerge, and often change during the lifetime of a collaborative design team.
- Constraints are always present in design activities, but collaborative designers use those constraints to creatively improve design ideas.
- Designers use collaboration to build and rebuild prototypes to envision and refine solutions.
- The changing nature of professional design is moving out of the realm of an individualized craft and into a collaborative process.
- Creativity is fostered through collaboration and collaboration cultivates creativity.
- Despite our practice of celebrating a singular "creative hero," most innovative work is done collaboratively.

Exercises to Cultivate Designer Collaboration

It is difficult to engage in exercises individually to cultivate your collaboration designer professional identity, so although we list a few here for you to reflect on individually, we encourage you to seek out collaboration opportunities to truly cultivate your collaboration designer professional identity development.

Looking at my behaviors: We discussed three behaviors you need to work on collaborative teams. Thinking about the three behaviors we highlighted in this segment – trust, respect, and willingness – reflect on the following:

1. List all the people you currently trust in your professional life. Now, look at that list. What actions do these people exhibit that result in your trust? Do you see these actions in yourself?

What do you need to do to develop these actions? If trust is something you feel you need to work on, how will you develop your behaviors so you will have professional trust in others, and they will have it in you?

2. Think about one person in your professional life that you respect. Why do you respect this person? What behaviors does this person exhibit that makes you respect them? When you reflect on your professional behaviors, do you believe people respect you? If so, why, or why not? What is one thing you need to work on to develop professional respect?

3. Think about the last time someone asked you to change your idea or decision to make a design better. What was your reaction to this request? How willing were you to let go of your idea knowing it might not develop the way you would have it developed if you worked alone? How willing are you to give up being a "creative hero" and be a part of a collaborative team? What behaviors do you need to be a willingness designer? What is one thing you are willing to do today to exercise your willingness muscle?

Exercises for Designers Who Teach

1. **What we share:** To find commonalities in your design team, divide the team into pairs and set a timer for two minutes and begin to list all the things each pair have in common. This can include shared hobbies, owning a pet, favorite foods, traveling, etc. When the two minutes are up, have each pair join another pair to compare lists to find commonalities with the now four people, striking the items that are not commonalities with all four and adding the ones that are. Depending on how large the team is, continue this process until you have a list of commonalities that the entire team possesses.

2. **What I bring:** Effective collaboration includes an understanding that each team member brings value to the team. Have each designer stand up and give an example of one moment in design that they are particularly proud of. This may include any design activity they have engaged in personally or professionally. This

activity will help all team members understand what each member brings to the team and create an atmosphere of respect. It also encourages team members to get to know fellow members skill a little better.

3. **Design on the fly:** Divide the group into small design teams of no more than three people. Assign each team a design problem and provide them with physical design materials including white board, sticky notes, etc. The team must determine and document their shared goal and use design materials to create a solution for their design problem within a given amount of time (decide on the time depending on the design problem you give the teams). The team must also come to consensus on their solution, then present it to the other design teams. All team members then vote on the best design solution to the problem.

Energy for Your Journey

Dialogue is 'playful'; it requires the willingness to play with new ideas, to examine them and test them. As soon as we become overly concerned with 'who said what,' or 'not saying something stupid,' the playfulness will evaporate, …

(Senge, 1990, p. 246)

References

Ball, L. J., Christensen, B. T., & Halskov, K. (2021). Sticky notes as a kind of design material: How sticky notes support design cognition and design collaboration. *Design Studies, 76,* 1–31. doi: https://doi.org/10.1016/j.destud.2021.101034

Beahm, G. (Ed.). (2011). *I, Steve: Steve Jobs in his own words.* Agate Publishing.

Bowen, S., Durrant, A., Nissen, B., Bowers, J., & Wright, P. (2016). The value of designers' creative practice within complex collaborations. *Design Studies, 46,* 174–198. https://doi.org/10.1016/j.destud.2016.06.001

Brereton, M. F., Cannon, D. M., Mabogunje, A., & Leifer, L. J. (1996). Collaboration in design teams: How social interaction shapes the product. In N. Cross, H. Christiaans, & K. Dorst (Eds.), *Analysing design activity.* Wiley.

Brown, T., & Katz, B. (2011). Change by design. *Journal of Product Innovation Management, 28*(3), 381–383. doi: https://doi.org/10.1111/j.1540-5885.2011.00806.x

Buchanan, R., Cross, N., Durling, D., Nelson, H., Owen, C., Valtonen, A., Boling, E., Gibbons, A., & Visscher-Voerman, I. (2013). Design. *Educational Technology, 53*(5), 25–42. https://www.jstor.org/stable/44430183%0A

Constantino, B., & Cho, J. Y. (2015). Calibrating collaboration: Strategies for creative output. *The International Journal of Design Management and Professional Practice*, *9*(3), 1–12. doi: https://doi.org/10.18848/2325-162X/CGP/v09i03/38631

Coulentianos, M. J., Rodriguez-Calero, I., Daly, S. R., Burridge, J., & Sienko, K. H. (2019). Medical device design practitioner strategies for prototype-centered front-end design stakeholder engagements in low-resource settings. *Proceedings of the Design Society: International Conference on Engineering Design*, *1*(1), 957–964. doi: https://doi.org/10.1017/dsi.2019.101

Cross, N. (2011). *Design thinking: Understanding how designers think and work*. Berg.

Dorst, K. (2003). *Understanding design: 150 reflections on being a designer*. Bis Publishers.

Du, J., Zhou, M., Xu, J., & Lei, S. S. (2016). African American female students in online collaborative learning activities: The role of identity, emotion, and peer support. *Computers in Human Behavior*, *63*, 948–958. doi: https://doi.org/10.1016/j.chb.2016.06.021

Gal, U., Blegind Jensen, T., & Lyytinen, K. (2014). Identity orientation, social exchange, and information technology use in interorganizational collaborations. *Organization Science*, *25*(5), 1372–1390. doi: https://doi.org/10.1287/orsc.2014.0924

Jacobs, G. (2017). 'A guided walk in the woods': Boundary crossing in a collaborative action research project. *Educational Action Research*, *25*(4), 575–593. doi: https://doi.org/10.1080/09650792.2016.1203344

Jordan, M. E., & Babrow, A. S. (2013). Communication in creative collaborations: The challenges of uncertainty and desire related to task, identity, and relational goals. *Communication Education*, *62*(2), 210–232. doi: https://doi.org/10.1080/03634523.2013.769612

Lawson, B., & Dorst, K. (2009). *Design expertise* (1st ed.). Routledge.

Reilly, R. R., Lynn, G. S., & Aronson, Z. H. (2002). The role of personality in new product development team performance. *Journal of Engineering and Technology Management*, *19*(1), 39–58. doi: https://doi.org/10.1016/S0923-4748(01)00045-5

Schwier, R. A., Campbell, K., & Kenny, R. (2004). Instructional designers' observations about identity, communities of practice and change agency. *Australasian Journal of Educational Technology*, *20*(1), 69–100. doi: https://doi.org/10.14742/ajet.1368

Senge, P. (1990). *The fifth discipline: The art & practice of the learning organization*. Doubleday.

Steane, J., Briggs, J., & Yee, J. (2020). T-shifting identities and practices: Interaction designers in the fourth industrial age. *International Journal of Design*, *14*(3), 85–96. http://www.ijdesign.org/index.php/IJDesign/article/viewFile/3728/914

Steen, M. (2013). Virtues in participatory design: Cooperation, curiosity, creativity, empowerment, and reflexivity. *Science and Engineering Ethics*, *19*(3), 945–962. doi: https://doi.org/10.1007/s11948-012-9380-9

Stull, C. L., & Blue, C. M. (2016). Examining the influence of professional identity formation on the attitudes of students towards interprofessional collaboration. *Journal of Interprofessional Care*, *30*(1), 90–96. doi: https://doi.org/10.3109/13561820.2015.1066318

Tracey, M. W. (2015). Design team collaboration with a complex design problem. In B. Hokanson, G. Clinton, & M. W. Tracey (Eds.), *The design of learning experience. Educational communications and technology: Issues and innovations* (pp. 93–108). Springer. doi: https://doi.org/10.1007/978-3-319-16504-2_7

Zamberlan, L., & Wilson, S. E. (2017). "Conversation leading to progress": Student perceptions of peer tutors' contribution to enhancing creativity and collaboration in a first-year design studio. *Journal of Peer Learning*, *10*, 59–75.

DECISION-MAKING

As a lead instructional designer, Makayla's design team was challenged to design and develop a building service excellence online course for an auto manufacturer's Mexico operations. The audience for the course was service department managers and service department technicians working at Mexico's dealership service departments. No problem thought Makayla. Her team had designed building service excellence courses for the automaker's U.S. operations. As a new online course, the Mexico dealerships had no design assets to share. Now, this was a problem. As Makayla looked around the table at her team, she casually dropped in the middle of the table the online course script, written in Spanish, that the Mexico City dealership had sent. Glancing once around the table, Makayla could see uncertainty in the eyes of the graphic designer, head programmer, course builder, scriptwriter, and head project manager. Thinking out loud, Makayla was blunt, "This one is going to take some creativity." The team began to reflect on what they had designed in the U.S. version of building service excellence. Finally, the graphic designer looked around the table and stated, "I could animate it." What? Animate a car dealership service department training course. This was something that had never been done by this design team. Before anyone could object, the graphic designer was at the whiteboard sketching out a storyboard. Makayla smiled, "Fifteen minutes ago we were drowning in uncertainty. That uncertainty spurred our creativity and reflection. Now, we have a starting design decision."

A design is made up of many chains of decisions, which are interconnected. Together chains of decisions result in a complicated network of interconnected decisions. Weaving a network of interconnected decisions takes reflection, accepting uncertainty, and creativity.

If you were backpacking in the Southwestern United States, your travels may take you to the coordinates – 36°59'56.325"N and 109°2'42.67"W. Here, you would find the Four Corners Monument that designates the quadripoint in Southwestern United States where the states of Arizona, Colorado, New Mexico, and Utah meet. The unique coordinates mark the only point in the United States shared by four states. You have reached the decision-making destination and a quadripoint in your designer professional identity travels where the four *segment* monument you stand before includes decision-making, reflection, creativity, and uncertainty. As you delve into decision-making, do not stand at the point where all four segments meet, get on your hands and knees and straddle the four – one leg in reflection, the other leg in decision-making, one arm in creativity, and the other arm in uncertainty.

One Decision, Two Decision, Three Decision, Four

You have been at a point where a design idea that you have been working on, moving forward step by step, turns into an already existing design or an idea that you already rejected. You get to the point because design decisions are dependent on one another; a decision you take from one part of your design affects the rest of the design (Dorst, 2003). A design is made up of many interconnected chains of decisions. Together chains of decisions result in a complicated network of interconnected decisions (Dorst, 2003). Weaving a network of interconnected decisions takes reflection, accepting uncertainty, and creativity.

Dorst (2003) explains that a design project begins with loose ends and we start by combining unconnected ideas into some type of whole. We never quite know whether a different starting point would have provided a, "...simpler web of decisions" (Dorst, 2003, p. 44). We keep moving forward connecting problems and ideas. We continually reflect on our evolving design solution because a decision that might solve a problem in one area could provoke a problem in another area (Dorst, 2003). Uncertainty sets in as we can begin to lose track of what we are doing. We take stock in our creative external representations and ask, "What was the reason for this" (Dorst, 2003)? Designers are good at weaving complicated webs of decisions.

How many decisions make up a complicated web? Stefaniak and Tracey (2014) asked 20 designers to describe a previous project and a decision they had made. In interviewing graphic designers, instructional designers, architects, and interior designers, Stefaniak and Tracey (2014) asked, "How many times did you review/refine the decision over other possibilities? Describe these iterations" (p. 90). The 20 designers followed one to 20 design iterations. Only six of the 20 designers cycled through two or less iterations. Stefaniak and Tracey (2014) concluded that designers, in any discipline, perform a balancing act of fluid decision-making, "...where designers cannot rush decisions but also cannot wait too long to gather necessary information" (p. 89).

What Does Straddling the Four Segment Monument Look Like?

We will do two things in this section. We will retell a design story and using brackets with italics highlight how the designers straddled decision-making, reflection, uncertainty, and creativity.

Tracey and Hutchinson (2018) present an interesting design story. A design team of four was challenged to come up with an instructional design intervention to teach adolescent girls attending a weeklong residential camp about bullying. Although none of the designers had ever used Twitter as an instructional tool [*uncertainty*], the team brainstormed the Twitter possibilities [*creativity impacting a decision iteration*]. The team was worried about the design constraints, the audience of campers, and the short one-week delivery cycle [*uncertainty*]. The team was confident in the vision they wanted to create for the campers [*creativity sparking a decision iteration*], but the challenges remained in discovering and refining [*decision iterations*] what the final learning experience would be.

To move forward in the design space [*creativity spurring a decision iteration*], the designers shared stories [*reflection*]. One designer shared her experience attending a similar one-week camp while another team member recalled being bullied as a child. A third designer described her extensive multimedia experience even though she was a Twitter novice. She suggested that she could transfer her multimedia design skills to the design situation [*reflection informs creativity which leads to a decision iteration*]. The fourth designer contributed that her strong knowledge of instruction and learning would be applicable. Regarding the tight deadline, all the designers had experienced short design timelines before and had diverse design experiences and believed that they had a responsibility to the campers to give them the best possible experiences [*uncertainty and reflection influence creativity which results in decision iterations*]. As a team, the designers felt confident [*face head-on the decision iterations*] in their ability to design a meaningful instructional intervention by relying on their collective expertise and experience [*reflected on*] to confront [*uncertainty of the design*] the unique constraints and opportunities [*creativity driving decision iterations*] present in the design situation.

Wouldn't it be nice if we could relieve the complexity of design challenges by breaking down the problem into smaller parts (Dorst, 2003)? Unfortunately, we usually cannot get to smaller parts because design problems have so many interrelated elements (Dorst, 2003). The problem-solution relationship for the bullying instructional design team was multilayered with the campers, the bullying topic, the one-week deadline, Twitter capabilities, and other constraints. Driving a meaningful instructional design, in part, was the how reflection, uncertainty, and creativity influenced the decision iterations.

How Do I "Twist" My Way in Understanding How a Web of Decisions Affect My Designer Professional Identity?

Have you ever played the game Twister? Twister has a Twister game mat with dots colored in red, green, blue, or yellow, and a spinner board divided into four parts: one for your left leg, right leg, right arm, and left arm. Each body part section includes the four colored dots. Spin the spinner! The person responsible for spinning the spinner calls out the color and which hand or leg to move (e.g., left hand red). All players must move their left hand to an empty red circle as quickly as possible. Only one foot or hand per colored circle. Spin again! The game continues and when your knee or elbow touches the mat or when you fall over you are out. Keep playing until there is only one player standing. Winner!

To better understand the relationship between decision-making and reflection, uncertainty, and creativity, we will play designer Twister. Stop straddling the four segment monument for a moment. Stand up and spin the spinner. You may want to revisit the reflection, uncertainty, and creativity segments before you move.

Left-Foot Decision-Making and Right-Arm Reflection

Schön (1983) described reflection-in-action as having a conversation with a design situation. As you reflect on the design situation, the situation talks back offering insight into the problem and solution. Decisions become binding as *what can* and *what might* happen turn to *what should* or *must* happen. In other words, design exploration becomes design commitments and possibility moves to imperatives (Schön, 1983). Design has a beginning, middle, and end. To meet the end date, designers make design decisions and commitments.

Mintzberg (2011) presents design exploration to design decisions through a reflection/action relationship. When speaking about the dynamic nature of a manager's (who are designers) job, Mintzberg (2011) stresses that managers must find time to step back and out when faced with a problem or opportunity. Reflection turns to action (decisions). Reflection without action is passive while action without reflection is thoughtless (Mintzberg, 2011). When developing the

International Masters in Practicing Management to allow managers to reflect with each other on their experiences, one manager coined the term "refl'action," which captures the need to combine reflection and action (Mintzberg, 2011). Mintzberg (2011) concluded, which we feel describes designers too, effective managers when faced with great pressure can cool it, just for a moment, to act thoughtfully. Possibility moves to imperatives.

Right-Foot Decision-Making and Right-Arm Uncertainty

In the uncertainty segment, you learned the importance of living with uncertainty. Your tolerance or intolerance for uncertainty affects your thoughts and emotions to make decisions. When you are uncomfortable with uncertainty, you put your energy toward reducing the uncertainty. As a result, you may make less wise decisions because reducing your uncomfortable feelings has become so important. In other words, if you work to avoid living with uncertainty you will spend a lot of time on information that will help reduce your discomfort level rather than focusing on information needed to design a meaningful deliverable. Cultivating your designer professional identity gives you a higher tolerance for uncertainty, which leads to effective decision-making. Fighting uncertainty hampers decision-making and creativity.

Left-Arm Decision-Making and Left-Leg Creativity

Design requires you to be creative and able to make decisions. You know from the creativity segment that creativity draws on both your thoughts and your emotions. Openness or open-mindedness provides you with the opportunity to be creative. Think about one or two of your toughest design projects. Would you agree that the tougher the design project, the more you had to be creative in your approach to the design problem? This is exactly how Makayla felt when she bluntly stated, "This one is going to take some creativity." When you are open to new experiences like Makayla's team creating an animated course for building service excellence, your designer curiosity increases along with your interest in getting your design teammates' ideas and insights. Creativity flows. When creativity flows *what can* and *what might* happen turn to *what should* or *must* happen. Creative design exploration becomes design commitment. Decisions are made and the design moves forward.

Takeaways: Decision-making

- A design is made up of many interconnected chains of decisions.
- Weaving a network of interconnected decisions takes reflection, accepting uncertainty, and creativity.
- Designers are good at weaving complicated webs of decisions.
- How reflection, uncertainty, and creativity influence decision iterations will help drive a meaningful instructional design.
- When we reflect-in-action, decisions become binding as *what can* and *what might* happen turn to *what should* or *must* happen.
- Developing your designer professional identity gives you a higher tolerance for uncertainty, which leads to effective decision-making.
- When creativity flows, *what can* and *what might* happen turn to *what should* or *must* happen.

Exercises to Cultivate Decision-Making

Design teams must make decisions. How decisions are made affect design team members' commitment to the life of and work of the team. Most design teams would benefit from skill practice in decision-making to train team members in what helps and what hinders good decision-making. Unlike other segments, here, we combine the individual designer exercises and exercises for designers who teach. These exercises were adapted from Christine Greishaber's *Step by Step Group Development – A Trainer's Handbook*. More details on these exercises can be found in Grieshaber (1994).

1. **The pool**: Give a group an experience of making a real decision or use an actual decision-making process, if there is one. Identify subgroups with opposite ideas. Representatives of each subgroup meet in the middle of the big group and discuss their ideas/options. The rest of the group carefully listens identifying ways how the decision-process can be improved.
2. **The pool (variation 1)**: Place a free chair among the representatives. Allow a member of the big group to come to the

middle and join the conversation. How have the discussion dynamics changed?

3. **The pool (variation 2):** Different options are discussed in the middle. Now, those who agree on the same point sit behind their representative. Limit the discussion to 10 minutes. After 10 minutes, the representative turns around to their subgroup and the subgroup expresses their thoughts on how to continue the discussion. It is also possible to change the representing person from round to round so all have a turn sitting in the middle. The 10-minute rounds continue until the participants think the topic has been discussed satisfactorily or a decision is to be made.

4. **Mapping the situation**: Form teams that work together in real design situations. Each team draws a map of their design situation on a piece of flipchart paper. The map includes every group, organization, and audience of focus in their design context that the team relate to, try to influence, work with etc. When the team had finished, the team asks the following questions:

   a.   Which of these groups or units are we really trying to influence?

   b.   How successfully are we doing this?

   c.   How good is the relationship within each group?

   d.   What areas do we have problems in?

   e.   How can we improve things?

Have each team tape their map to the wall and have all participants walk around and review the maps. After all have viewed the maps, allow anyone with questions to ask the team.

Energy for Your Journey

Too much reflection and nothing gets done; too much action and things get done thoughtlessly.

(Mintzberg, 2011, p. 215)

References

Dorst, K. (2003). *Understanding design: 150 reflections on being a designer.* Bis Publishers.

Grieshaber, C. (1994). *Step by step group development: A trainer's handbook.* Deutsche Stiftung für Internationale Entwicklung.

Mintzberg, H. (2011). *Managing.* Pearson Education, Inc.

Schön, D. A. (1983). *The reflective practitioner: How professionals think in action.* Basic Books, Inc.

Stefaniak, J. E., & Tracey, M. W. (2014). An examination of the decision-making process used by designers in multiple disciplines. *TechTrends, 58*(5), 80–89. doi: https://doi.org/10.1007/s11528-014-0789-7

Tracey, M. W., & Hutchinson, A. (2018). Reflection and professional identity development in design education. *International Journal of Technology and Design Education, 28,* 263–285. doi: https://doi.org/10.1007/s10798-016-9380-1

CLOSING
THE JOURNEY CONTINUES

Each day, Makayla rises and anticipates looking at the world as a designer. She continues to embrace uncertainty when starting a new design. She has discovered new ways of communicating and collaborating with her design teams while they create ethical inclusive deliverables. Committing to the importance of ongoing learning while being empathic toward herself and her audience, Makayla has devised a creative means of learning something new every day continuing to cultivate her designer professional identity. As Makayla steps out on her daily design journey, she eagerly smiles knowing that this is a journey that will continue, and continue, and continue and...

What I call Professionalism someone else might call the Artist's Code or the Warrior's Way, It's an attitude of egolessness and service. The Knight of the Round Table were chaste and self-effacing. Yet they dueled dragons, ...

(Pressfield, 2002, p. 108).

 DOI: 10.4324/9781003255154-12

What a journey visiting all ten segments. Your trip has provided you with a window into your designer professional identity. You know where you are now, where you are heading, and how you can continue to cultivate your designer professional identity. Breathe deeply, stretch tall, and relax as we revisit where you have been so far.

A Brief Review of Your Membership

By engaging in your designer journey, you are becoming the master of cultivating your designer professional identity. As a member of the design community, each segment on this trip has provided you with an opportunity to gain a new perspective, find a new approach to a design situation and reflect on your designer growth. Like Makayla, you understand that this journey is far from over, but you now have a map to help you continue to cultivate your professional identity. This book is your journey map where you moved from segment to segment cultivating your designer professional identity. Let's revisit the stops you made.

Your empathy visit provided you with an introduction to empathy as a design approach. You learned that empathy is an inborn ability as well as a learned skill. The highlight of this stop on your journey was the practical activities to aid you in developing empathy for your audience of focus, for yourself, and for the localized context of use.

Your journey brought you to the uncertainty segment where you explored uncertainty as both an essential and routine part of design. You were given a framework for developing your designer professional identity which embraces uncertainty. You discovered your relationship to uncertainty and were given practical techniques to recognize, accept, and embrace uncertainty in design as necessary for creativity, innovation, and curiosity.

When you took some time at the creativity segment, you explored creativity in designer professional identity as a combination of internal processes and external practices that are environmentally situated, embodied in actions, and cultivated through purposeful nurturing. You discovered perspectives on expanding sources of inspiration as your designer professional identity develops, while being encouraged to recognize emotions as an integral part of your creative professional identity. You were given techniques to cultivate your designer creativity, harness emotions as a source of innovation, and integrate creativity into collaborative design work.

You were challenged in the ethics segment to consider your design impact on the social, political, and natural environment. You experienced insight on how ethical design aims to promote well-being, giving people an opportunity to live as they like in a sustainable way, and enhances social innovation. You discovered that the development of your ethical designer professional identity is a resolution of the internal intentions and external manifestations of design.

The diversity, equity, and inclusion segment provided you with an opportunity to explore design as an expression of radical empathy that moves your audiences and you toward actions that promote more than just outcomes. Harnessing your designer introspection, interaction, and intention to identify the most critical forces will help you to form a localized context of use while designing, supporting your efforts in diversity, equity, and inclusion. You discovered your ability to transform situations of inequity, lack of diversity, and exclusion by influencing your everyday choices.

Traveling through the reflection segment, you explored the role of reflective conversations between you as the designer, the design problem, and tentative solutions. You realized that developing your designer professional identity includes design as an explicitly reflective practice while your implicit reflective skills are nurtured through experiences. You recognized that reflection is a conceptualization of your personal and internal knowledge construction through recursive considerations and interpretations of your experiences and beliefs.

When you stepped into the learning segment, you explored design as an active process of learning and recognized that learning is a vital process for you to develop your designer professional identity. You discovered that formal education, practice, and reflection are interrelated components of learning and development. Finally, you realized that learning from failure provides you with a vital opportunity for your personal and professional growth.

When your trip landed you in the communication segment, you discovered the overview of communication and its reciprocal relationship to designer professional identity development. Your insight into different theories of communication included the basic forms of communication, the role of listening in effective design communication, and the essential communication functions for design. You embraced the practical tools to improve listening and communication skills that contribute positively to your collaborative design process.

You stopped in the collaboration segment and explored design as a fundamentally collaborative effort, where you interact with other designers' skills, ideas, experiences, and opinions in pursuit of a common goal. You discovered the impact of collaboration on creativity and the relationship between collaboration and your professional identity development.

Twisting in the decision-making segment, you synthesized creativity, uncertainty, and reflection to explore the web of interrelated decisions that build a meaningful design and your designer professional identity. You reflected on the perspectives on decision-making as iterations that flow from abstract possibilities to practical imperatives in realizing a design. You experienced the practical examples of designers embracing uncertainty to make creative decisions that are enriched by careful reflection.

Your Professional Identity Journey Continues!

You continue to journey, and this journey map is here for you to revisit repeatedly. You are encouraged to go back to the segments whenever you want to further cultivate a particular skill. Maybe you are having a difficult time experiencing empathy for an audience you are designing for; then it is time to revisit the empathy segment. Are you stuck in a design problem and can't create a viable solution? If so, it is time to revisit the creativity segment. Maybe you are part of a design team that doesn't seem to be relating to one another, looks like you need to jump into the collaboration segment. Wherever you are, whatever you are designing, your guide will be there to help you navigate your designer professional identity.

Identity appropriately refers to *becoming*, meaning that your work in cultivating your professional identity is constant. When you wake in the morning, you may choose to turn to your design journal and reflect on actions you took the day before alone or in your design community.

As you experience your day, you will gather tidbits of information, experiences, and memories that will support your continued designer development. Knowing that the main source of continuous designer professional identity development is through design projects, you will immerse yourself in all forms of design, learning from each experience while developing your designer expertise. We wish you the very best on your journey. Keep designing!

Energy for Your Journey

We're not born with unlimited choices. We can't be anything we want to be. We come into this world with a specific, personal destiny. We have a job to do, a calling to enact, a self to become. We are who we are from the cradle, and we're stuck with it.

Our job in this lifetime is not to shape ourselves into some ideal we imagine wo ought to be, but to find out who we already are and become it, …

(Pressfield, 2002, p. 146).

Reference

Pressfield, S. (2002). *The war of art: Break through the blocks and win your inner creative battles.* Warner Book.

For Product Safety Concerns and Information please contact our EU
representative GPSR@taylorandfrancis.com
Taylor & Francis Verlag GmbH, Kaufingerstraße 24, 80331 München, Germany

* 9 7 8 1 0 3 2 1 5 3 1 4 8 *